DIRECTIONS, PLEASE

Kenneth D. Barney

RadiantBOOKS 🔴))》
Gospel Publishing House/Springfield, Mo. 65802

02-0856

Library of Congress Catalog Card Number 83-82080
International Standard Book Number 0-88243-856-5
Printed in the United States of America

A teacher's guide for individual or group study with this book is avail-
able from the Gospel Publishing House (order number 32-0197; ISBN
0-88243-197-8).

Contents

1

Pentecost Is Now

READ JOHN 14:16-20,26; 15:26,27; ACTS 1:1-14

Why is it so important that I be aware of my relationship to the Holy Spirit?

The vital consideration is what the Bible has to say about this great truth. What did Jesus, our highest authority, teach about the Holy Spirit's ministry to believers?

With just a few hours to impart His final instructions to the men who would lead His church, Jesus gave them His most extensive teaching about the Holy Spirit. John records it in chapters 14,15, and 16 of his Gospel.

The word Jesus used to speak of the Holy Spirit is translated "Comforter" in the King James Version of the Bible. Other versions use different words. The *New American Standard Bible* and the Williams' New Testament both say "Helper." The New International Version reads "Counselor." All of these translations are actually correct. Together they help us understand who the Holy Spirit is and what He does.

The Greek word translated "Comforter" is *parakletos*, meaning one called alongside to help. Frequently we anglicize it as "Paraclete."

Jesus said the coming of the Spirit would be the result of His personal petition to the Father (John 14:16). He

5

called the Spirit *another* Comforter. Why "another"? Because Jesus had been their Comforter, Helper, Counselor, Paraclete, and now He was about to return to heaven. A Comforter like Him was coming to teach and lead the disciples as He had. The Comforter would be unseen by natural eyes, but His presence would be no less real than that of Jesus.

The announcement of Jesus' departure was a blow to the disciples, but He assured them they would not be forsaken. The Holy Spirit was not coming temporarily. He would stay with His people forever (John 14:16).

Jesus then used another term further describing the Holy Spirit: "The Spirit of truth." The Spirit of Truth would teach Jesus' followers the whole truth. He would explain and interpret the Word of God for them. He would enable them to discern teaching that was *not* true, thus safeguarding them from error.

A New Era

Jesus' promise in John 14:17, "He dwelleth with you, and shall be in you," shows that the disciples had something to look forward to. Before Jesus' death and resurrection the Holy Spirit was "with" the disciples but he was not an abiding presence in their lives. Their new relationship must await the death, resurrection, and ascension of Jesus Christ. This is the meaning of John 7:39: "The Holy Ghost was not yet given; because that Jesus was not yet glorified."

In a few weeks the "with" would be changed to "in." After Pentecost the Spirit would indwell believers, making their bodies His temples (1 Corinthians 3:16; 6:19; 2 Corinthians 6:16).

"I will not leave you comfortless," Jesus promised (John 14:18). The Greek word for "comfortless" is *orphanos*, from which we get "orphan." The Saviour literally said to those heavyhearted men, "I will not leave you orphans."

With the coming of the Holy Spirit the disciples would understand their relationship to Jesus and His relationship to the Father (John 14:16,20). He had explained these matters to them before, but they had not grasped His teaching (John 16:12). It would be different when the Spirit of Truth came. The disciples' minds would be enlightened; their spiritual understanding expanded.

In John 14:23 Jesus continued His teaching about the intimate fellowship between God and His children after the coming of the Holy Spirit: "If a man love me, he will keep my words: and my Father will love him, and we will come unto him, and make our abode with him."

God making His home in His people—this is the miracle of the Spirit's indwelling. No longer would the Lord stay at a distance as He did at Sinai while He gave the Law. Even when the tabernacle was constructed, no one but the high priest could go behind the veil where the outward manifestation of God's presence hovered over the mercy seat. And the high priest could enter only once a year.

The Schoolmaster's Work Finished

As strange as some of the rituals of the Law seem to us, God was working out His purpose in those days. He was leading mankind toward the day when Jesus would appear. But man was not ready yet, for he was in his spiritual childhood.

Paul makes an interesting statement in Galatians 3:24, calling the Law a schoolmaster. He declares that the schoolmaster's task was to bring us to Christ.

The Law emphasized the impossibility of sinful man approaching a holy God. The sinner had to come with a blood sacrifice, and he needed a priest as his intermediary. The priest in turn had to offer sacrifices for his own sin (Hebrews 7:26,27). Fellowship with God in those days was enjoyed by only a few.

Joshua (Numbers 27:18), Micah (Micah 3:8), and David (1 Samuel 16:13), for example, had strong relationships with God. But now the prospects of a relationship with God would go beyond natural boundaries. It would happen after Christ's work of redemption had been accomplished. Then Jesus would return to heaven and present His petition to the Father for the gift of the Spirit to be poured out on His followers—"as many as the Lord our God shall call" (Acts 2:39).

The schoolmaster's work was almost done. Jesus was about to die as the perfect sacrifice for sin, and no more animals would have to be offered on altars. The commandments of God which had been written on stone would now be written in the believers' hearts (Hebrews 8:7-10).

Jesus' remaining hours with His disciples were few. There was not time to tell them everything they needed to hear; they would not have understood anyway. But now the Saviour gave them another great promise:

> These things have I spoken unto you, being yet present with you. But the Comforter, which is the Holy Ghost, whom the Father will send in my name, he shall teach you all things, and bring all things to your remembrance, whatsoever I have said unto you (John 14:25,26).

The Holy Spirit would be a Teacher as well as a Helper. The minds of the disciples could not contain everything Jesus had told them during his 3 years with them. But the Holy Spirit would quicken their minds and the disciples would continually remember and understand the truths that had slipped into their subconscious. The Spirit would explain and interpret every lesson the Master had presented. What a Teacher!

It's for Us Too

The Spirit's teaching ministry would also involve truths Jesus had not brought to the disciples; the Spirit would teach them "all things."

In John 16:13 Jesus promised the Spirit would guide believers "into all truth." This shows us the Spirit's concern that we involve ourselves with the whole balanced picture of truth. If we are sensitive to His voice he will help us avoid being so occupied with one portion of truth that we acquire a distorted view. How wise and skillful this Teacher is, and how carefully He guides us in the path of righteousness as we wait for the return of our Saviour.

Only a small number of people actually heard Jesus speak, but the Spirit would guide some of them in recording His teachings. These writings would become part of the Scriptures, and as long as the Church is on earth the Spirit will use the Bible as His textbook to instruct every one who accepts Jesus as Saviour.

What a privilege to be taught by the Spirit day by day. It is our privilege today just as much as it was the blessing of those in the Early Church. We rightly call the present age the dispensation of grace and the Church Age. It is also the age of the Holy Spirit.

Of course there never was a time when the Holy Spirit was not present on earth, for He is one of the Godhead. But at Pentecost He came to God's people in a special, unique way. His mission is not only to call out men and women from sin and build Christ's church, but also to guide and instruct every Christian in the truths on which the Church is founded.

In John 14:26 we note the involvement of all three

members of the Trinity in the promise Jesus was making: Jesus speaks of "the Comforter, which is the Holy Ghost." He refers to the Father. And, speaking of himself, Jesus says the Spirit would come "in my name."

In John 15:26 we see another instance of the Trinity's presence: "But when the Comforter is come, whom I will send unto you from the Father, even the Spirit of truth, which proceedeth from the Father, he shall testify of me."

Glorifying Jesus

Coming in Jesus' name meant that the Spirit would be concerned with glorifying and honoring that Name. He would focus on the name of Jesus and lift it up. The Spirit abides in God's people to call the world's attention to one name—*Jesus.*

Jesus reinforced this truth by a further statement in John 16:13,14: "He shall not speak of himself. . . . He shall glorify me: for he shall receive of mine, and shall show it unto you."

How important it is to remember that as much as we appreciate the feelings we experience from the Spirit's presence in our lives, these feelings are not to be exalted above our relationship with Christ. The Spirit did not come to call attention to what He does for us, but to help us keep our eyes on the Lord Jesus.

After Jesus finished the work of His atonement and defeated death by His resurrection, He spent 40 days with His disciples before returning to His Father's right hand (Acts 1:1-3).

When the hour of His ascension arrived, the disciples certainly seemed like a different group. They bore little resemblance to the sorrowing men who had been with Jesus just before His crucifixion. (See Luke 24:46-53; Acts 1:1-14).

The disciples knew now that Jesus was victor. They would have been happy to keep Him with them, for they stood gazing into the heavens after He ascended. Apparently they hoped He might return. But they obeyed His command to stay in Jerusalem until they were "endued with power from on high." His praises were on their lips continually.

Jesus called the coming of the Spirit "the promise of my Father." The Father had given many promises, but this one was special, unique. The mission of the Church depended on it. Unless the Spirit came it would be useless for the disciples to try to carry on Christ's work.

Pentecost—Just the Beginning

The disciples did not know the exact day the Spirit would be poured out on them. But they did what Jesus commanded, and gathered in an upper room to pray and wait.

On the Day of Pentecost (the Old Testament Feast of Weeks) it happened. The Church was launched on its age-long mission. Throughout the Book of Acts the Spirit's presence overshadowed everything the Christians did. He so empowered ordinary men and women that the Church's enemies were baffled and defeated.

How glad we are that in his sermon at Pentecost Peter made it clear that the gift of the Spirit is for Christians in every age—including us:

Repent, and be baptized every one of you in the name of Jesus Christ for the remission of sins, and ye shall receive the gift of the Holy Ghost. For the promise is unto you, and to your children, and to all that are afar off, even as many as the Lord our God shall call (Acts 2:38,39).

The disciples realized they were not working alone.

11

They recognized the Spirit's presence and power as they prayed and preached. In Acts 5:32 Peter declared: "And we are his witnesses of these things; and so is also the Holy Ghost."

When seven men were chosen to oversee the Church's welfare program and keep the burden off the disciples' shoulders, one requirement for those men was that they be full of the Holy Spirit (Acts 6:3). When one of the men, Stephen, became the first Christian martyr, one of the last things said about him as he faced his tormentors was that he was full of the Holy Spirit (Acts 7:54,55).

When the apostles at Jerusalem heard the news of the revival in Samaria, they sent Peter and John to that city to pray that the new converts would receive the Holy Spirit (Acts 8:14-17). The powerful presence of the Spirit exposed the true nature of a sorcerer who was trying to attach himself to the Church (Acts 8:9-24).

After the conversion of the Church's fierce persecutor, Saul of Tarsus, he was filled with the Spirit and thus empowered for his great ministry as the apostle Paul (Acts 9:17-19).

When Peter preached to the Gentiles of Cornelius' household, he was convinced of their salvation when the Holy Spirit fell on them and they spoke in tongues just as the Jewish believers had done on the Day of Pentecost (Acts 10:44-48).

Paul and Barnabas were called by the Holy Spirit as the Church's first missionaries (Acts 13:2-4).

When Paul found at Ephesus disciples of John the Baptist who had not heard about the Holy Spirit, he instructed them, prayed for them, and they were filled with the Holy Spirit, speaking in tongues and prophesying (Acts 19:1-7).

It is this way throughout the Book of Acts. The Holy

Spirit dominates every page of this record of Early Church history.

To the End of the Age

The last Book of the New Testament, Revelation, discloses the tremendous events at the end of this age, culminating in the new heavens and the new earth. John was able to write this Book because he was "in the Spirit" (Revelation 1:10).

The messages John sent to the seven churches were from the Spirit (Revelation 2:7,11,17,29; 3:6,13,22). The Spirit will not abandon His people during the cataclysmic events of the end time. He will empower and sustain them until the victory is won. He will continue lifting up Jesus before this sinful world.

At the close of the Book of Revelation, the Holy Spirit and the Church join in an invitation to a lost, dying world, "Come" (Revelation 22:17). How necessary it is that the Church's voice always harmonize with the voice of the Spirit.

Today, Christians of many denominations are being baptized in the Holy Spirit. This is the way God intended it. The blessing of the Spirit's infilling is not for a favored few. It is for the whole Church. Have you claimed this promise of Jesus for yourself?

2

The "Bread Alone" Syndrome

READ LUKE 12:13-34; JAMES 4:13-16

What's wrong with getting everything you can while the getting's good? You live only once, don't you?

This philosophy is summed up by a word we hear frequently: *materialism.* It means a preoccupation with material things to the neglect of spiritual matters. The materialist is so concerned about his body that he gives little thought to his soul. His attention is taken up with this present world and he rarely thinks about the life to come. Time is everything to him. Eternity doesn't matter. Nor does God or His Word or His church.

A Property Dispute

In Luke 12:13-34 the Bible records one of Jesus' most potent lessons on materialism. It started because a man in His audience was upset over the settlement of an estate. Interrupting Jesus' teaching, the man implored Jesus to put pressure on his brother to give him a fair share of the property their father had left them.

Perhaps the man was justified in his complaint. His brother may have been a greedy rascal who had cheated his own flesh and blood. But Jesus saw that the man was so preoccupied with his financial problem that spiritual teaching meant little to him.

Jesus came straight to the point: "Beware of covetousness." (Luke 12:15).

However legitimate the man's claims may have been, Jesus detected the monster of greed ready to pounce on him. So the Saviour said, "Watch out. Be careful." The warning is just as much for us as it was for the man standing in front of the Saviour that day.

We Aren't Just Bodies

In a brief sentence Jesus summed up a powerful truth: "A man's life consisteth not in the abundance of the things which he possesseth" (Luke 12:15).

Our possessions are not what life is all about. To be concerned only about money, property, stocks and bonds, houses, automobiles, boats, etc., is to assume that the only important part of us is our body.

When Jesus was tempted by Satan to make bread out of stones, He quoted an Old Testament verse that declares: "Man shall not live by bread alone, but by every word that proceedeth out of the mouth of God" (Matthew 4:4). He was emphasizing this truth to the distraught man in His audience that day.

We must have bread. Our physical needs are real. But a "bread alone" philosophy will separate us from God. We have a spiritual nature too, and it must be nourished by His Word. Few people would starve their bodies by doing without food, but many starve their spirits by neglecting the Word of God.

The Rich Fool

This was a great opportunity for more teaching on this vital subject, and Jesus took advantage of it. He told a story about a successful farmer who had such good crops that he was running out of storage space. (See Luke 12:13-21.) He stayed awake nights—not thinking about

15

how he would glorify God with his wealth, but worrying about his barns being too small.

Jesus was not criticizing success or implying that it was evil to raise good crops. But as we follow the story we detect a complete lack of spiritual priorities in this man's thinking. He was obsessed with what he had accumulated in this present world—and he hoped to continue accumulating.

The man's decision was made. He would demolish the barns he had and replace them with bigger ones. But the fatal flaw in the man's character showed up in this bit of midnight musing: "I will say to my soul, Soul, thou hast much goods laid up for many years; take thine ease, eat, drink, and be merry" (Luke 12:19). The *Good News Bible* words it this way: "Then I will say to myself, Lucky man! You have all the good things you need for many years. Take life easy, eat, drink, and enjoy yourself!"

Isn't this a picture of people you know today? God is left out of their thinking, their planning, their desires. "Grab, grab, grab" is their philosophy. "More, more, more" is the incessant cry of their inner nature.

God Interrupts

But the rich farmer's reverie was suddenly interrupted. Although he had forgotten God, God had not forgotten him. The Lord said that He was closing the books on the man's life before morning. The man would never see the light of another day. Then what would happen to all those things he had labored so hard to accumulate?

God's greeting to the farmer was, "Thou fool!" Strong words. Not very polite or tactful. But that's the label God puts on the materialist: FOOL!

Jesus concluded His story by warning that the fate of

this man would be shared by anyone who piles up riches for himself but "is not rich toward God."

God Will Take Care of You

Jesus' teaching was always beautifully balanced (Luke 12:22-31). He continued the lesson by assuring His disciples that God is concerned about the physical well-being of His children. They should not fret about having enough to eat and wear, for their Heavenly Father has promised to take care of them. Jesus observed that there is more to life than food and clothes. His followers must keep such matters in perspective.

Jesus reminded the disciples that the birds they were so familiar with were the object of the Father's care. The birds did not plant crops and had no barns where they could store their food supply, but God feeds them. Since God's children are worth more than birds, why should they spend time worrying about where their food is coming from?

Then Jesus referred to a flower that also was common to his hearers. He declared that even King Solomon's gorgeous robes could not compare with the flowers. Who gave them such stunning beauty? The same God who feeds the birds.

But flowers are here only for a little while, Jesus reminded His listeners. If God takes care of the beauty of flowers, why should His children be distraught about what they will wear? Then the Master injected a slight rebuke—which many of us also deserve at times: "O ye of little faith" (Luke 12:28).

Things

"Things" is the theme of Jesus' ongoing lesson. "All these things do the nations of the world seek after" (v. 30). He was talking about pagans or unbelievers. "Things"—provisions for the physical part of life—were all they were concerned about. But lest anyone should think that God is not mindful of our day-to-day necessities, Jesus said, "and your Father knoweth that ye have need of these things" (v. 30).

Then what should our attitude be toward "things"? Jesus put it plainly: "But rather seek ye the kingdom of God; and all these things shall be added unto you" (v. 31).

Here is an eternal principle. If we concern ourselves first with God's plan, His purpose, and His will, we can be sure he will provide us with the "things" that occupy all the time and attention of unbelievers. We will not starve or be naked. We will be able to pay our bills. We will be provided for. God will see to it. Just be careful to keep Him first—not second or third or fourth.

Jesus reassured His listeners that although they were a "little flock" compared with those opposed to Him, they would inherit an everlasting kingdom. This promise is to Christians today as much as then.

Heavenly Treasure

Jesus counseled His disciples to provide themselves with the kind of purses that would not wear out. The purses men carry will not hold "a treasure in the heavens"—the wealth "that faileth not" (Luke 12:33). Thieves can steal earthly wealth, but they cannot touch our heavenly treasure.

Inflation, taxes, and other financial enemies reduce what we amass for ourselves on earth. But the treasure we are putting on deposit in heaven by our service to God can never lose its value.

In Luke 12:34 Jesus stated an unchanging principle that covers life in every place and time: "For where your treasure is, there will your heart be also."

On the surface these words may seem a simple truth, but the more you consider them the more profound they become. It is human nature to put our best efforts into what interests us most. We automatically pay the greatest attention to what we value most. If we are forced to give some attention to matters that do not greatly interest us, we are only halfhearted about it. Our real love gets our best.

You do not have to be around people very long to discover where their treasure is. Their affections and deep dedication gravitate to that treasure. There is no way for them to conceal what has really captured their hearts.

This is not the only Scripture passage concerning materialism. The Bible is full of such passages. James 4:13-16 says a lot about materialism:

> Go to now, ye that say, Today or tomorrow we will go into such a city, and continue there a year, and buy and sell, and get gain: whereas ye know not what shall be on the morrow. For what is your life? It is even a vapor, that appeareth for a little time, and then vanisheth away. For that ye ought to say, If the Lord will, we shall live, and do this, or that. But now ye rejoice in your boastings: all such rejoicing is evil.

James is describing people who are much like the rich fool in Jesus' parable. They are not wrong in making business plans, but their attitude is arrogant and self-centered. These people act as though they are the masters of their own destinies, that they can decide how much time they have in this world.

Unfortunately, buying, selling, and getting gain are all these folks think about. They are blind to heavenly treasures. Their strategy is all for this world alone.

James asks a good question: "What is your life?"

(v. 14). What is it? Our view of life will not only determine the course we take while here on earth, but it will also decide our eternal future.

James' illustration of life is striking. Life is like a puff of steam. Now you see it; now you don't. Compared to eternity, that's just how long life is. To spend all of it making plans only to buy, sell, and get gain will make us lose everything.

In verse 15 we are cautioned to temper our planning with the provision, "If the Lord will." This will keep us humble. It will remind us that we are responsible and accountable to Someone. The Lord will someday close our books and audit them. We will be called upon to give an account of our lives.

Let's Claim the Promise

The apostle Paul kept his balance and maintained the right perspective on material things. In Philippians 4:12 he wrote: "I know both how to be abased, and I know how to abound: every where and in all things I am instructed both to be full and to be hungry, both to abound and to suffer need."

Paul was certain that God would supply not only all of his needs, but also those of the Philippians to whom he was writing: "But my God shall supply all your need according to his riches in glory by Christ Jesus" (Philippians 4:19). You and I can claim this promise just as much as the first readers of this Epistle.

God does not assure His people that they will be wealthy. We are not guaranteed a life free of bumps, jolts, and financial problems. But the Lord does promise that He will meet all our needs. Not all our wants and whims, but all our needs.

The guarantee of this promise is "his riches in glory,"

bestowed on us through our Lord Jesus Christ. What more could anyone ask?

The apostle Paul saw life as Jesus said we should see it. He maintained the right set of values and trusted God to take care of his earthly needs while he concentrated his attention on the riches of eternity.

Materialism—Everyone's Enemy

One of the saddest occasions in Jesus' ministry occurred when a man we commonly call the rich young ruler turned and walked away from the Master. Why this strange behavior? He had learned that following Jesus would mean giving up his wealth (Matthew 19:16-30).

The Saviour does not often make such a demand, and many Christians have used their wealth for God's glory. Apparently the Lord saw that the young ruler's riches would always be a spiritual problem, so He made a severe demand on him which was rejected.

But materialism is not a problem only for the rich. Many who are not wealthy have just as serious a struggle maintaining the right attitude toward "things." They do not become rich, but they are obsessed with getting more and more. They become very attached to what they gain.

Some Christians find it difficult to tithe. Overcoming selfishness is a never-ending struggle when we are battling for financial independence.

"If riches increase, set not your heart upon them" (Psalm 62:10). It is that "setting of the heart" that becomes a man's downfall. It is the "trust" in riches that Jesus said makes it hard for people to enter the kingdom of God (Mark 10:24). Such trust makes it easy for us to absorb the spirit of the Laodicean church: "I am rich, and increased with goods, and have need of nothing" (Revelation 3:17).

Paul felt it necessary to exhort Timothy: "Charge them that are rich in this world, that they be not high-minded, nor trust in uncertain riches, but in the living God" (1 Timothy 6:17).

Few things require more self-discipline than handling financial prosperity in a manner pleasing to God. The Lord does not condemn ambition or success. He does not tell us He is displeased if we make a good salary. But His Word warns us to stay alert to the danger always lurking in the accumulation of material possessions.

If we are blessed financially, let us thank God for it and dedicate our possessions to Him. If we do not seem destined to be wealthy, let us not exhaust ourselves trying to reach such a goal. Life is indeed like a puff of steam, and when that vapor disappears someone else is going to claim what we worked so hard to get. When our time of departure comes, we need to be sure that on the other side of the grave we have amassed a fortune we can enjoy forever.

3

God's Rules Haven't Changed

READ 1 SAMUEL 12:1-4; PROVERBS 11:3; 16:11

Can we still apply Biblical teachings to life in our times? Is it practical to practice honesty and fair play in a society where competition is so fierce?

Our beloved America has been experiencing a moral breakdown in recent years. It hasn't happened overnight. Such things never do. The tragedy has been building up for a long time and finally has emerged into the open.

The whole moral fabric of the nation seems to be unraveling. The symptoms are not limited to one segment of society. They are everywhere, and sometimes they appear to encircle us.

The area of politics has received much of the attention as far as this problem is concerned. The chicanery of some men elected to positions of public trust has made cynics of many. But the pall also hangs over the business world, the educational system, the home, and sometimes even the religious world.

Integrity is talked about frequently these days, yet it seems to have suffered a tremendous delcine.

The Bible Teaches It

The Bible often focuses on the word *integrity*. In the King James Version the word itself does not appear in the New Testament, but it occurs 16 times in the Old Testament. Basically the Hebrew word translated "integrity" means "completeness."

In both the Old and New Testaments there are many passages that talk about integrity without actually using the word.

Webster's New Collegiate Dictionary has several definitions of integrity. One of them is "completeness," which agrees with the meaning used in the Bible. The dictionary also says integrity means firm adherence to a code of moral values. This is a good definition, but we must understand that true integrity is not mechanical. It goes beyond a mere observation of rules. The quality of integrity is woven into a person's character. It is what he really is.

What we are determines what we do and how we act and react in the various situations of life. If we lack integrity, this character flaw will show up sooner or later. We may cover up for a while, but a time will come when we will experience the kind of pressure that will expose the real self.

Proverbs 11:3 says: "The integrity of the upright shall guide them: but the perverseness of transgressors shall destroy them."

The integrity of the upright gives them a soundness that keeps them from going to pieces under the pressure of temptation. Instead of doing something crooked or underhanded, they have a strength of purpose that keeps them doing what is right in the sight of the Lord.

How different is the ultimate outcome of the life where integrity is absent. "Perverseness" means crookedness.

In today's world it may seem that crookedness pays better than integrity. But the Bible gives us the whole picture. It shows us the final destiny of people. Eventually the crooked life will bring about its own destruction. It will fall under the weight of its own sin.

No Other Guidebook

The rules on integrity are found in one book, the Bible. Don't look to the world around you for guidelines.

Some people may laugh at you for believing in the Bible, but it has stood the test of time and its standards do not change. What does a little ridicule matter if we know we are following the Lord's directions?

Integrity should begin with an individual's relationship with God; however, spiritual completeness must come first. Integrity starts with the fear of the Lord and the knowledge of His will. Without these one is not a complete person.

Integrity toward God means that we do not try to "use" Him for our own selfish purposes. We should serve God because it is right to serve Him and sinful to do otherwise. It is disconcerting to see people make strong resolutions to serve God when they are under pressure, only to forget their commitments to God when the trial has passed.

Integrity toward God will lead us to ask concerning our actions, "Would this be displeasing to Him?" Some worldly philosophies ask only, "Can I get by with it? Will it make me popular with the right people? Will it build up my bank account?"

These Men Had Integrity

Joseph was far from home. A lustful woman was trying constantly to seduce him. One day a perfect opportunity to have an affair presented itself: no one would be the wiser. To her repeated advances Joseph emphatically declared, "How . . . can I do this great wickedness, and sin against God?" (Genesis 39:9). No human eye would have seen them, but God's eye would have, and that was what really mattered to Joseph.

Daniel was also in a foreign land. He had been taken to Babylon when that nation conquered Israel. The king recognized the young Jew's potential as a government servant. An intended part of Daniel's training involved "a daily provision of the king's meat, and of the wine which he drank" (Daniel 1:5).

This would have been a violation of God's law. Although he was removed from the surroundings of his early life, "Daniel purposed in his heart that he would not defile himself with the portion of the king's meat, nor with the wine which he drank" (Daniel 1:8).

Of course Daniel risked the possible loss of a profitable career. Conceivably he could have been executed for disobeying the royal decree. But that was secondary to this man of integrity. As you know from reading the Book of Daniel, his firm stand was vindicated. God blessed him and gave him a position in the government that survived even the fall of the king.

Godly integrity will keep us from engaging in wrongdoing with the idea that we will ask God to forgive us when it's all over.

Integrity in Business

Integrity is no more severely tested than in the business world. This is an arena where competition is merciless. It is often bare knuckle, no-holds-barred combat. Must a Christian adopt the tactics of the world to succeed in business? Will he go broke if he tries to operate according to Biblical standards? Do nice guys really finish last?

Proverbs 16:11 declares: "A just weight and balance are the Lord's: all the weights of the bag are his work." Here's another way of wording it: "The Lord wants weights and measures to be honest and every sale to be fair" *(Good News Bible)*.

That's plain enough, isn't it? Simple—but plain. And it is God's own rule. A man may appear to succeed for a time by breaking the rule, but what about in the long run? What is he doing to his own conscience, character, and personality? What about the hour when he stands before God at the judgment?

When the elderly Samuel spoke to his nation he asked the people to declare whether they had ever known him to cheat or take advantage of anyone. What a tribute the people paid the godly old man: "Thou hast not defrauded us, nor oppressed us, neither hast thou taken aught of any man's hand" (1 Samuel 12:1-4).

Can you think of a greater reward than having people say this about you after knowing you for a lifetime? Doesn't such a testimony make the "rewards" of dishonesty look cheap?

In our day we have heard so many stories about businessmen taking bribes and making under-the-table deals that sometimes we are not even shocked. Such tainted money may buy a lot of things someone wants, but it also distorts his conscience and destroys his relationship with God. And what about self-respect? To be able to look at yourself in the mirror with a clear conscience is no small reward.

Cheating is often a game that people play against each other. It is considered sport to outsmart the other cheater. The rationale is, "Everybody else is doing it, so why shouldn't I make my share when I can?"

Such thinking, of course, ignores God and His Word. It overlooks the truth that God has appointed a day when

He will judge the world in righteousness (Acts 17:31). There will be no appeal from His verdict.

Honest Workmen

When King Joash was engaged in repairing the temple, he gave money to craftsmen for the work. What a testimony we have of the integrity of those workmen: "The men in charge of the work were thoroughly honest, so there was no need to require them to account for the funds" (2 Kings 12:15, *Good News Bible*).

What kind of business world would we have today if everyone in it possessed the integrity of those ancient carpenters, stonecutters, and masons?

John the Baptist had some interesting things to say on this subject. One day, after John warned the crowd that baptism required a change in behavior, some tax collectors and soldiers asked him, "What shall we do?" To the tax collectors he said, "Exact no more than that which is appointed you" (Luke 3:12,13). This is completely opposite to the present philosophy of many in the commercial world: "Charge what the traffic will bear."

To the soldiers John said, "Do violence to no man, neither accuse any falsely; and be content with your wages" (Luke 3:14). This counsel to working men balanced beautifully what had just been said to management. Wouldn't it be wonderful if all business dealings were conducted in that kind of atmosphere?

Do You Have a Price?

There is a cynical saying, "Every man has his price." It is the belief that no matter how honest and upright an individual may be, he has a point at which he would be willing to sell out his convictions.

Unfortunately, we have publicly witnessed such compromises of principle. We are left disappointed and

28

sometimes shaken. May such a lapse of integrity never be true of anyone who calls himself a follower of Jesus Christ!

When Naaman, the Syrian captain, was healed of his leprosy, he was so grateful for Elisha's prayers that he wanted to reward him. But Elisha had firm convictions about accepting pay for his ministry. He refused the offer.

But Elisha had a servant named Gehazi, and his integrity cracked at this point. All Gehazi could think of was the wealth he and Elisha could have acquired for the asking. Quickly he devised a scheme and ran until he caught up with Naaman's departing chariot.

Gehazi had a convincing story about some unexpected guests who needed money and clothes. Naaman was glad to oblige, and Gehazi left with two fine suits of clothes and two bags of silver.

But Elisha was in touch with God and knew what had happened. Gehazi's punishment for his betrayal of trust was to be stricken with leprosy, which he would pass on to all his descendants (2 Kings 5:20-27).

Of course the loss of integrity doesn't ordinarily result in contracting leprosy. Sometimes it appears that there is no punishment at all. But beware! No one can break God's laws with impunity. When a person throws away his convictions and sinks to the level of the ungodly, something happens immediately on the inside of him. He may not realize it at once, but in his personality, his thinking processes, his spiritual sensitivity, an erosion begins. He is not quite the same person as he was. Outwardly it may not be evident at once, but time will show cracks in the foundations of his character. It isn't worth it for one to lose his integrity.

Blessed Are the Clean

Who shall ascend into the hill of the Lord? Or who shall stand in his holy place? He that hath clean hands, and a pure heart; who hath not lifted up his soul unto vanity, nor sworn deceitfully. He shall receive the blessing from the Lord, and righteousness from the God of his salvation (Psalm 24:3-5).

During sacred seasons such as the Passover, the ancient Jews chanted Psalm 24 as they climbed the hill of Moriah to the temple.

Ultimately the "hill of the Lord" is heaven. But even while we are on earth we can enjoy communion with the Lord which is a foretaste of that future day. However, not everyone is going to heaven, and not everyone can have fellowship with God.

"Clean hands" are hands that are not involved in sin. They stay clean because the heart that motivates the actions is pure. Jesus promised: "Blessed are the pure in heart: for they shall see God" (Matthew 5:8).

"Hath not lifted up his soul unto vanity" (Psalm 24:4) refers to the worship of idols. We do not worship idols made of wood, metal, or stone, but there are many people who lust after things that are just as worthless.

To swear deceitfully means to make false promises. Unfortunately this is how many people get ahead. Their word means nothing. They lie with a straight face to promote their own selfish aims.

Which do we want—the fleeting "rewards" that seem to come from sinful living, or the rewards that God bestows on those who live by His Word?

4

Beyond the Grave—What?

READ 1 CORINTHIANS 15

Why does there have to be death? How can we find reliable information about what happens after death?

Paul calls death an enemy (1 Corinthians 15:26). Who would disagree with him?

In recent years we have seen an attempt to bring death into the open and view it more objectively. Some colleges even offer classes about death and how to cope with it.

We bring as much beauty and comfort to the funeral service as we can. Cemeteries now are usually the memorial garden type with flat markers and a look of peacefulness.

Yet the heartbreak of death remains. Even if we are expecting it because a loved one is terminally ill, death still hurts when it comes.

For a Christian to grieve over the loss of someone dear is natural. But the believer has an advantage the unsaved do not possess. The Christian believes in a Book that contains much teaching about the subject of death. It shows him why death exists and discloses what happens after death. For the child of God, the Bible is full of hope and encouragement in the face of death.

When Did It Begin?

When God created man He did not intend that man should ever die. But since God made man a free moral agent He tested him to see if he would be obedient. Adam and Eve were told not to eat the fruit of the tree of the knowledge of good and evil. God said: "In the day that thou eatest thereof thou shalt surely die" (Genesis 2:17). This is the first time the word "die" appears in the Bible.

Unfortunately, Adam and Eve made the wrong decision. They listened to the devil and partook of what God had forbidden. Because of this they lost their innocence and their fellowship with God. They became sinners and passed on a sinful nature to every human ever born— except Jesus. Along with the sinful nature came physical death as well as other curses which are still seen everywhere.

Paul underscores this tragic truth in 1 Corinthians 15:21,22: "By man came death. . . . In Adam all die."

Adam and Eve were driven away from the tree of life, which would have kept them alive forever (Genesis 3:22-24). After that, it is not long until we read of death. The first death was a murder, a fratricide (Genesis 4:8).

The 5th chapter of Genesis is a roll call of the dead, starting with Adam. A brief summary is given of each individual's life, ending always with the words, "and he died." The one exception is Enoch, who without dying was simply taken to heaven by God. In this chapter we also notice that as time went on the human life span gradually became shorter.

If we are puzzled because an ugly thing like death is present in a world that God created, the Bible gives a clear answer. Death is here because sin is here. Nothing could be plainer than Paul's statement in Romans 5:12:

"Wherefore, as by one man sin entered into the world, and death by sin; and so death passed upon all men, for that all have sinned."

Let's Stay With the Word

In recent years a number of books have been written about life after death. Most of these deal with the reported experiences of individuals who believe they died and came back to life.

Some of these testimonies may be the genuine experiences of Christians. Other testimonies are dangerous because they imply that whether a person has been a follower of Christ in this life or not, he need not worry about judgment. We should be cautious; these stories invariably picture a being of warmth and light who is apparently indifferent to the kind of life one has lived and is ready to receive everyone into eternal bliss.

The Bible is the only trustworthy authority about life after death. Experiences like those mentioned above are subjective and must be scrutinized in light of scriptural teaching. Whatever may be the explanation of these varied experiences that would eliminate man's acountability to God, the Bible states emphatically: "It is appointed unto men once to die, but after this the judgment" (Hebrews 9:27).

The Christian and Death

The Bible divides the human race into two groups— the saved and the lost. There is no neutral ground, no in-between position. Everyone is either on God's side or the devil's depending on one's acceptance or rejection of Jesus Christ, the only Saviour.

The Christian can look at death with faith and courage because Jesus has conquered death. When He died on the cross as the one perfect sacrifice, the sins of the world were placed on Him. "For Christ also hath once suffered for sins, the just for the unjust, that he might bring us to God" (1 Peter 3:18).

When we accept Jesus as our Lord and Saviour, we are forgiven and sin loses its power to dominate us. God then can consider us righteous because the righteousness of His Son is deposited to our account.

Death also loses its power over us when we are saved. If Jesus does not return first, our bodies will die but our spirits will go immediately into God's presence. When Jesus comes our bodies will be raised, glorified and made immortal, to join our redeemed spirits in heaven.

Hebrews 2:14,15 focuses on this truth of Jesus' bringing "many sons to glory":

> He . . . shared in their humanity so that by his death he might destroy him who holds the power of death—that is, the devil—and free those who all their lives were held in slavery by their fear of death (New International Version).

Victory!

For the Christian no passage of Scripture sounds a more victorious note about death than 1 Corinthians 15, the great resurrection chapter. The concluding verses are like an anthem:

> Behold, I show you a mystery; We shall not all sleep, but we shall all be changed, in a moment, in the twinkling of an eye, at the last trump: for the trumpet shall sound, and the dead shall be raised incorruptible, and we shall be changed. For this corruptible must put on incorruption, and this mortal must put on immortality. So when this corruptible shall have put on incorruption, and this mortal shall have put on immortality, then shall be brought to pass the saying that is written, Death is swallowed up in victory. O death, where is thy sting? O grave, where is thy victory? The sting of death is sin; and the strength of sin is the law. But thanks be to God, which giveth us the victory through our Lord Jesus Christ (1 Corinthians 15:51-57).

In 2 Corinthians 5:1-9 Paul discusses the Christian's death in an interesting way. (See the *Good News Bible*.) He compares death to taking down a tent (our physical body) and moving into a permanent home (our immortal body).

Paul also uses the illustration of clothing. He speaks of the new body as a new suit of clothes which he looked forward to putting on over the old worn-out clothing of mortality.

The Bible does not tell us everything we might like to know about the body we shall receive in heaven, but we read in Philippians 3:20,21 that it will be patterned after the glorified body of our Saviour.

The Book of Revelation tells us the most about our eternal home, especially in the last two chapters. There will be no more death. Pain, tears, and all of sin's other by-products will be forever absent.

The Christian's hope of victory over death is one of the great blessings brought to us by the gospel. It enables us to face death, not with stoicism, hopeless grief, or bitter resignation, but with faith, joy, and peace. Death is not a pleasant subject, but the child of God can view it from a Biblical standpoint. He is comforted by Jesus' promise: "Because I live, ye shall live also" (John 14:19).

Death and the Unbeliever

The Bible speaks of three kinds of death: spiritual, physical, and eternal.

Adam and Eve did not die physically as soon as they disobeyed God. In fact Adam lived several more centuries. We have no record of Eve's life span. But they died spiritually as soon as they broke God's law.

The Bible describes people who have not accepted

Christ as "dead in trespasses and sins" (Ephesians 2:1,5; Colossians 2:13). As a dead person cannot respond to those around him, so the sinner cannot respond to God. His spiritual nature is dead. All have sinned (Romans 3:23), and all are spiritually dead until they are brought to life by turning to Christ.

For the Christian, everlasting life begins when he is saved. Heaven is simply a continuation of a never-ending life that even physical death cannot destroy. For the sinner, existence in the next world is a continuation of the death that already has him in its grip. He leaves his earthly body and continues to die—forever. If an individual persists in sin, no other outcome is possible: "The wages of sin is death" (Romans 6:23).

Those who criticize "hellfire-and-brimstone preachers" should be aware that no one ever preached about hell in such clear and somber language as Jesus.

Mark 9:42-48 is a striking example. Jesus said that if a person's hand or foot would cause him to be lost he would be better off without it than to go to hell. He said if a person's eye causes him to sin, it would be preferable to reach heaven with one eye instead of going to eternal damnation with two.

The Greek word translated "hell" in these verses is *geenna*, usually spelled Gehenna. Gehenna was the city dump. Fires were constantly burning there to destroy the refuse. Because of the presence of garbage and dead carcasses, the place was also crawling with worms.

Jesus used Gehenna as a picture of the everlasting punishment of sinners. "Where their worm dieth not, and the fire is not quenched" (v. 48)—these are Jesus' own words. The "worm" probably refers to the unrelieved gnawing of the sinners' conscience.

What a picture! Thrown on the garbage dump of the universe to rot forever, away from everything beautiful, pleasant, and uplifting. Above all, forever away from God and surrounded with degradation and corruption.

Two Who Died

In Luke 16:19-31, Jesus told of two men who died. On earth their positions were a stark contrast, for one was a beggar and the other very rich. Their state after death was even more opposite. The beggar was carried by the angels to his eternal reward, but the destiny of the rich man was very different.

Jesus said: "The rich man also died, and was buried" (v. 22). But this was not the end, for "in hell he lifted up his eyes, being in torments" (v. 23). The lost soul was fully conscious and in possession of all his faculties, including speech and memory. He recalled his life on earth and was in agony over the possibility of his brothers coming to that terrible place.

Worst of all, the rich man was aware of the beggar's enjoyment of peace and comfort, for he was able to see Lazarus "afar off" (v. 23). But the two were forever separated by "a great gulf" (v. 26).

There is no way to gloss over the Bible's teaching about the eternal punishment of the unsaved. It is not pleasant to think about, but hell is the only possible end for a sinful life. According to Jesus, hell was prepared for Satan and his fallen angels, but those who serve the devil must follow him there (Matthew 25:41).

Forever Is a Long Time

After the final judgment the wicked will be cast into their permanent place of torment, the lake of fire. This ushers them into a state the Bible calls the second death (Revelation 20:14,15). It is not annihilation or a cessation of consciousness, for we remember that after being cast into the lake of fire a thousand years before, the beast and the false prophet are still there (Revelation 20:10).

To die forever—it is beyond the comprehension of the natural mind. To be fully conscious and aware of one's surroundings in a place of utter misery, suffering, and despair defies all human description. The condition of those in that place can hardly be called life, so the Bible calls it death—the second death. If an individual dies without Christ, another death still awaits him.

No one needs to be lost, for it is God's will that all should be saved (2 Peter 3:9). If a person is lost, it is in spite of God's love and work on his behalf. Those who go to hell must ignore the Cross and dismiss the love of Jesus Christ.

For the Christian, death—although its coming brings heartache—is a defeated enemy. All believers will share Christ's victory over death. When a Christian is finally absent from the body he will be present with the Lord (2 Corinthians 5:8). Why would anyone want to make any other choice except to turn to Jesus and live forever?

"The wicked is driven away in his wickedness: but the righteous hath hope in his death" (Proverbs 14:32).

5
Why, God? Why?

READ JOB 38; 39

Why do the innocent suffer? Why do the righteous suffer? Why does God permit evil and suffering at all? Many people find these questions difficult and distressing.

In this chapter we will use the term *suffering* in a broad sense, since it can include many things. Much suffering is physical—the result of sickness, accidents, or criminal assaults. But emotional and mental suffering can be just as intense as physical pain.

Suffering may come from financial pressure or family difficulties. It may involve situations over which we have no control and in which we are innocent victims. Natural disasters often contribute to human misery. There is no end to the different directions from which suffering can overtake us.

Human nature wants quick, simplistic answers to problems. Suffering is a complex subject, and each situation has its own puzzling questions. A blanket solution to suffering is not possible. Some answers will *never* come until we stand in God's presence. However, at that time we may have forgotten why the answers seemed so necessary.

In this study we will not pretend to answer every

question about suffering. We will focus on several facts concerning the subject and attempt to give Biblical guidance in those areas. We pray the Holy Spirit will use this teaching to comfort, encourage, and strengthen those people whose faith may be sorely tried by the dilemma of suffering.

Suffering Is Universal

There is nowhere in the world to hide from suffering. It may have more severe manifestations in some places, but in one form or another suffering follows us all from the cradle to the grave.

Why? Because we live in a world that is under the curse that began when man became a sinner by his disobedience to God. Sickness, pain, suffering, and death afflict the human race because man is a rebel against God's laws.

The hatred, jealousy, greed, and violence that often cause suffering are the products of depraved, fallen human nature.

On our TV screens we have seen the terrible ravages of wars in various places. The toll of human misery in our time is incalculable. God did not create the world in this condition; it is the result of man's sinful nature.

We have felt the anguish over genocidal acts of totalitarian governments. Refugees number in the millions around the world, and their plight is unbelievable.

The victims of suffering are often innocent. They may be Christians. The plight of those victimized by war and hunger is a challenge to the compassion of all mankind. We cannot stand idly by and fail to do everything possible to alleviate their torment.

God's ultimate plan calls for the elimination of every aspect of the curse (Revelation 22:3), but that time has not yet come. Until it does, every human—righteous or unrighteous, innocent or guilty—is exposed to the danger of living in a world where suffering stalks all mankind.

Don't Be Surprised

Our personal suffering should not surprise us. Paul says: "There hath no temptation [test] taken you but such as is common to man" (1 Corinthians 10:13).

Peter writes: "Beloved, think it not strange concerning the fiery trial which is to try you, as though some strange thing happened unto you" (1 Peter 4:12). When we feel the pressure of a trial it seems it has never happened to anyone else in quite the same way. We view it as a strange, or unusual, experience. Not so, says Peter. These things have happened to many and will continue to do so.

Sometimes God intervenes miraculously and wards off calamities. Sometimes He does not. If we had our way, He always would. It is easy for us to envision a world in which we as Christians are forever shielded from all the unpleasantness that happens to others. But we must be realistic. It does not happen this way, and the Bible does not teach us that it will.

Sin May Be the Cause

Some suffering comes because of personal sin. In the Old Testament we read of untold suffering by the nation of Israel when they turned from God to worship idols and follow the ways of the heathen. God allowed the Children of Israel to endure 70 years of captivity in Babylon. He sometimes used cruel foreign rulers to punish them.

It may be that the United States is undergoing trouble today because the majority of its people have turned their backs on God to go their own sinful way. In 2 Chronicles 16:9 God warned King Asa that because of his foolish disobedience, "from henceforth thou shalt have wars." Could there be a parallel here to our own beloved nation?

Individuals as well as nations may suffer because of their sin. "Whatsoever a man soweth, that shall he also reap" (Galatians 6:7). This is an immutable spiritual law. So is the warning of Numbers 32:23: "Be sure your sin will find you out." There is no way to break God's laws without getting hurt.

Suffering for the Lord's Sake

Jesus was "a man of sorrows, and acquainted with grief" (Isaiah 53:3). He told His disciples that He "must suffer many things, and be rejected of the elders, and of the chief priests, and scribes, and be killed, and after three days rise again" (Mark 8:31).

Peter writes: "For Christ also hath once suffered for sins, the just for the unjust, that he might bring us to God" (1 Peter 3:18).

The Saviour made it plain that becoming identified with Him would bring an individual into conflict with the world, resulting at times in personal suffering. He warned: "Ye shall be hated of all men for my name's sake" (Matthew 10:22). This hatred may express itself savagely. Throughout the centuries Christians have been brutalized, imprisoned, and killed for their loyalty to Jesus Christ. In some places this is still happening.

Jesus said concerning Saul of Tarsus, who became the apostle Paul, "I will show him how great things he must suffer for my name's sake" (Acts 9:16).

Hebrews 11 reviews some of the Old Testament heroes of the faith. Many of them were miraculously delivered from their enemies. But there was another group concerning whom the writer speaks quite differently:

And others had trial of cruel mockings and scourgings,

yea, moreover of bonds and imprisonment: they were stoned, they were sawn asunder, were tempted, were slain with the sword: they wandered about in sheepskins and goatskins; being destitute, afflicted, tormented; of whom the world was not worthy: they wandered in deserts, and in mountains, and in dens and caves of the earth (Hebrews 11:36-38).

These people suffered because they were godly. Unlike other godly folk, they were not spared. Yet despite this, they remained unflinchingly loyal to the Lord they loved.

God's School of Hard Knocks

Christians may suffer as a part of God's schooling. Scripture has some wonderful teaching along this line in Hebrews 12:7-11:

If ye endure chastening, God dealeth with you as with sons; for what son is he whom the father chasteneth not? But if ye be without chastisement, whereof all are partakers, then are ye bastards, and not sons. Furthermore, we have had fathers of our flesh which corrected us, and we gave them reverence: shall we not much rather be in subjection unto the Father of spirits, and live? For they verily for a few days chastened us after their own pleasure; but he for our profit, that we might be partakers of his holiness. Now no chastening for the present seemeth to be joyous, but grievous: nevertheless, afterward it yieldeth the peaceable fruit of righteousness unto them which are exercised thereby.

If God puts us through suffering, He does it because He loves us, not because He is trying to break us. He is exercising the same wisdom as a human father, who knows that a life free of discipline produces weak character.

A verse of Scripture often quoted but apparently not too well applied is Romans 8:28: "We know that all things

43

work together for good to them that love God, to them who are the called according to his purpose."

We should underline the two words, "all things." This includes the pleasant and the unpleasant, the blessings and the tests, sunshine and shadow—"all things."

Some of the "things" that come our way may not be good themselves. But this Scripture passage teaches us that God will make them *work* for our good. Some other translations may be helpful in understanding the full significance of this promise:

"We know that in all things God works for the good of those who love him" (New International Version).

"We know that God causes all things to work together for good to those who love God" *(New American Standard Bible).*

"We know that to those who love God, who are called according to his plan, everything that happens fits into a pattern for good" (Phillips).

Whatever happens to us we should realize we're not alone: God is with us and so are members of His family. Many Christians have been encouraged and sustained by witnessing the steadfastness of fellow believers during a trial. Paul was able to comfort those who were going through severe tests because he had been through the same experiences and had found God faithful (2 Corinthians 1:3,4).

What About Job?

Probably the best known figure associated with suffering is Job. He had three so-called friends who had everything figured out. They knew why he was going through such terrible trials: it was because he had sinned! For several days they pounded poor Job with their sanctimonious philosophy. When God appeared on the scene, near the end of the Book of Job, He came to Job's defense and rebuked his "friends" for criticizing a righteous man.

Sometimes we hear it said that the Book of Job answers the question, "Why do the righteous suffer?" This evaluation is not entirely accurate. No clear-cut answer is given Job to the problem of his suffering. What happened at the end of the book was this: God confronted Job with some interesting questions. Beginning with chapter 38, here are a few examples:

"Where wast thou when I laid the foundations of the earth?" (Job 38:4).

"Hast thou entered into the treasures of the snow?" (Job 38:22).

"Gavest thou the goodly wings unto the peacocks? or wings and feathers unto the ostrich?" (Job 39:13).

Of course Job had to answer no to these questions. The Lord was trying to help Job understand that since He was able to create and sustain the universe without his help, Job should be willing to trust Him with the details of his own life.

Couldn't Job leave the dilemmas to a Creator whose wisdom was far beyond his? If God could set the planets spinning and take care of His animal creation, didn't He have the power to watch over Job no matter what occurred?

This is the right attitude for us to have when unexplainable events, including suffering, disturb our serenity. If God can keep the world going we can surely trust Him with our lives.

Out of Job's trials came some of the most encouraging Scripture passages in the Old Testament. They have sustained many other "Jobs" during dark days. Open your Bible to the Book of Job and read them: Job 1:21; 13:15; 19:23-27; 23:8-10.

We would not have these beautiful words of faith if Job had not lived for a time in the crucible of suffering.

God indeed made all things work together for Job's good. Job's trials brought glory to God, clearer spiritual understanding to Job, and encouragement to God's children for all time to come.

God Will See Us Through

For the Christian, suffering is temporary. Paul—himself a sorely tried believer—wrote: "For I reckon that the sufferings of this present time are not worthy to be compared with the glory which shall be revealed in us" (Romans 8:18).

To the Corinthians Paul testified:

> For our light affliction, which is but for a moment, worketh for us a far more exceeding and eternal weight of glory; while we look not at the things which are seen, but at the things which are not seen: for the things which are seen are temporal; but the things which are not seen are eternal (2 Corinthians 4:17,18).

And don't forget Psalm 34:19: "Many are the afflictions of the righteous: but the Lord delivereth him out of them all."

When the going gets rough, try this Scripture passage:

> When thou passest through the waters, I will be with thee; and through the rivers, they shall not overflow thee: when thou walkest through the fire, thou shalt not be burned; neither shall the flame kindle upon thee (Isaiah 43:2).

When we suffer, we are assured of the compassionate understanding of a Saviour who has been through suffering too. He is "touched with the feeling of our infirmities." His testing while on earth was "in all points" like our own testing (Hebrews 4:15).

One of the last things Jesus said to His disciples before

returning to heaven was: "Remember, I am with you always, day by day, until the close of the age" (Matthew 28:20, Weymouth). This is a personal promise directed to every child of God in every circumstance, good or bad.

We are not left without resources in the time of suffering. Nothing will strengthen us more than the promises of the Bible. We will come through the wilderness of suffering with our faith stronger than ever if we hold tightly to the promises of the Word. Don't forget the lifeline of prayer. Powerful, prevailing prayer has kept many Christians on their feet when Satan was trying to knock them out through suffering.

Thank God for the support of fellow Christians. Don't isolate yourself when you are walking a dark valley. Develop a fellowship that is closer than ever with your brothers and sisters in Christ. Don't stay home from church to nurse your wounds in sullen loneliness. God's house is a place where strength is renewed as we worship and hear the Word preached and taught. Hold on to the shield of faith and quench those fiery darts of the enemy (Ephesians 6:16).

6

Satan's Well-Worn Tool

READ 1 KINGS 18:21; PSALM 42; ISAIAH 40:28-31

Isn't it natural to doubt? Is there any harm in always wanting an explanation for things we don't understand? Does that displease God?

Doubt is not a recent invention. It is as old as the human race. In the Garden of Eden Satan injected doubt into the minds of Adam and Eve about God's word, leading them to sin.

To doubt is to waver in our opinions; to be unsure of our convictions. The doubter is like the Israelites of Elijah's day. These people halted between opinions, unable to decide whether to serve God or Baal (1 Kings 18:21).

Doubt often arises when we apply human reason to spiritual truths. We are surrounded by the natural; our physical senses keep us very much in touch with our material world. This often makes it difficult to maintain our faith. We don't need to make an effort to cultivate doubt; it comes all too easily.

Our best weapon against doubt is the Bible. Paul calls it "the sword of the Spirit" (Ephesians 6:17). The Bible is a supernatural Book and is the true source of faith (Romans 10:17). Prayerful meditation on the truths of the Word keeps us on God's wavelength.

To the natural mind, doubt is almost automatic and

faith in God is impossible. Paul makes this clear in 1 Corinthians 2:14: "The natural man receiveth not the things of the Spirit of God: for they are foolishness unto him: neither can he know them, because they are spiritually discerned."

In this verse, "know" means to perceive, to understand clearly. The Christian who studies the Bible as a part of his daily life will not be a captive of the natural (spiritually unenlightened) mind.

A Common Problem

It is helpful to know that we are not the first ones who have struggled with doubt. In Psalm 42 the Psalmist asks himself the question: "Why art thou cast down, O my soul? And why art thou disquieted in me?" (v. 5) "Cast down" and "disquieted"—accurate pictures of a child of God fighting to maintain faith in the face of adverse circumstances.

But the Psalmist quickly finds the answer to his problem and exhorts his soul, "Hope thou in God." In verse 6 the Psalmist tells the Lord about his dilemma: "O my God, my soul is cast down within me." But he adds, "Therefore will I remember thee." In these two verses we have some simple but practical exhortations on dealing with doubt: (1) hope in God and (2) remember God.

The struggle was not over, for in verse 9 the Psalmist says: "I will say unto God my rock, Why hast thou forgotten me? Why go I mourning because of the oppression of the enemy?" Deep in his heart this man knew God never forgets His own. But the pressure of the trial made it easy for him to entertain the thought of being abandoned. Yet he still considered God his "rock." He was shaky, but the Rock wasn't.

The psalm ends on a note of victory, as the Psalmist repeats what he had already discovered: "Why art thou cast down, O my soul? And why art thou disquieted within me? Hope thou in God: for I shall yet praise him, who is the health of my countenance, and my God" (v. 11). This adds another spiritual dimension to hoping and remembering. Now we have praise—a glorious way to deflect our doubts.

Faulty Perception

Believing is not always easy. The more complicated and difficult a situation, the harder it is to exercise faith.

When the Lord promised Abraham and Sarah a child in their old age, Sarah actually laughed (Genesis 18:9-12). Again the cause of doubt was faulty perception. She was trying to apply natural reasoning to a supernatural promise. At Sarah's age, it was impossible to have a child, and her laughter showed she had not considered that God could intervene. But God did intervene, and the "impossible" became a reality when Sarah held baby Isaac in her arms.

Gideon, the man famous for defeating a large army with 300 men, did not always exercise faith. He was threshing wheat in a concealed spot when the angel of the Lord found him and greeted him with the words: "The Lord is with thee, thou mighty man of valor" (Judges 6:12)

At that moment Gideon was anything but a mighty man of valor, and present circumstances could not convince him that God was with him. He asked a natural question: "If the Lord be with us, why then is all this befallen us?" (Judges 6:13).

Such a question didn't end with Gideon. What Christian hasn't asked the same question today when the going has been rough?

Gideon recalled the stories he had heard of the times God had performed miracles of deliverance for His people. "Where are all those miracles now?" Gideon cried. "Why don't they happen anymore? We're in bondage to the Midianites because God has forsaken us."

God proved to Gideon that the day of miracles was not past and that He had not forsaken His people. He changed Gideon the doubter into a man of confidence and made him the instrument of deliverance from the Midianites. As Gideon took steps of faith, the Lord gave him victory—over both his doubts and the Midianites.

Don't Be Your Own Prisoner

We sometimes pray for something and then think of reasons why the answer won't come. This is making ourselves prisoners of our own intellect.

At times during Isaiah's ministry, the whole nation of Israel was crushed by doubts. Through the prophet the Lord asked the question: "Why do you say, O Jacob, and complain, O Israel, 'My way is hidden from the Lord; my cause is disregarded by my God'?" (Isaiah 40:27, NIV). This shows that the people believed God didn't even see their troubles, or if He did He was ignoring them.

The Lord gave the doubting people a fresh promise to lift their sagging spirits:

> Hast thou not known? hast thou not heard, that the everlasting God, the Lord, the Creator of the ends of the earth, fainteth not, neither is weary? there is no searching of his understanding. He giveth power to the faint; and to them that have no might he increaseth strength. Even the youths shall faint and be weary, and the young men shall utterly fall: but they that wait upon the Lord shall renew their strength; they shall mount up with wings as eagles; they shall run, and not be weary; and they shall walk, and not faint (Isaiah 40:28-31).

That's the secret—waiting on the Lord. Spend time

in His presence through prayer with His Word open before you. Remind yourself of His promises and His past goodness to you. Your strength will then be renewed; doubt will give way to faith, and you will be able not only to cope with your problems but to rise above them.

Another passage in Isaiah shows how tenderly God deals with His children during their times of doubting: "But Zion said, 'The Lord hath forsaken me, and my Lord hath forgotten me' " (Isaiah 49:14). There it is again—the feeling that somehow God had forgotten. But listen to the Lord speak in the very next verse: " 'Can a mother forget the baby at her breast and have no compassion on the child she has borne? Though she may forget, I will not forget you' " (v. 15, NIV).

God was reminding His people (and us) that His love surpasses even that of a mother. He does not stand ready to strike us because of our doubts, He reaches out His strong hand to lift us up and help us.

When the Bottom Falls Out

One of the classic Old Testament passages about a believer's attitude toward bad circumstances is Habakkuk 3:17-19:

> Although the fig tree shall not blossom, neither shall fruit be in the vines; the labor of the olive shall fail, and the fields shall yield no meat; the flock shall be cut off from the fold, and there shall be no herd in the stalls: yet I will rejoice in the Lord, I will joy in the God of my salvation. The Lord God is my strength, and he will make my feet like hinds' feet, and he will make me to walk upon mine high places.

Habakkuk was painting a picture where the bottom had fallen out of everything. Crops and herds were the main source of income for the Israelites, and to lose all of these would be a devastating blow. But the prophet declared that even if such a calamity happened he would rejoice. He was not a stoic gritting his teeth and trying to ignore the problems. He saw beyond the despair of the moment. His faith grasped the hand of the God of eternity. His spiritual perception was working. Doubt had no place in his thinking.

Of all people to have doubts, who would have thought John the Baptist would be a victim? He was filled with the Holy Spirit even before he was born. He shook the nation of Israel with his mighty preaching, announced the coming of the Messiah, and then boldly identified his own cousin, Jesus of Nazareth, as that Messiah.

But circumstances changed. Instead of being out in the desert preaching, John found himself one day in prison. During this confinement, he sent two of his disciples to ask Jesus if he really was the Messiah (Luke 7:19).

Jesus did not condemn John; He reassured him. He sent the disciples back with instructions to tell John about the miracles that were happening in Jesus' ministry. When John heard this he would know that his preaching had been true, that his mission had not failed, and that he was indeed God's man. The words of Jesus have a way of erasing doubt and causing faith to be reborn in our hearts.

We will probably never go to prison like John, but the day may come when we are cut off from church services and Christian fellowship by circumstances we cannot control. Broken health, for example, can create such a situation. Or we may have to move to a different part of the country, giving up familiar surroundings. In our time of adjustment to new conditions we may succumb to the temptation to miss church and make no effort to find new Christian friends. We may experience doubts.

Is our experience with the Lord real, or have we imagined much of it? Have we been foolish to try so hard to be spiritual? Doubts, doubts, doubts.

Hearing His Voice Again

What we need most of all at such a time is to hear again the clear voice of our Saviour. We *will* hear it if we keep our minds full of the Word and allow the Holy Spirit to keep us spiritually sensitive. Doubts may reappear, but we will be able to win the victory over them.

Probably one of the best known doubters in the Bible is the apostle Thomas. Among many students of the Word he has acquired the unfortunate title, "Doubting Thomas."

When Thomas heard that Jesus was risen from the dead, he flatly stated that until he could see Him for himself he would not believe (John 20:24,25). He had never seen anyone rise from the dead. How could it be possible? He knew Jesus had died, so how could He be alive now? In Thomas' discouragement, he completely forgot Jesus' promises about rising again.

But Thomas' doubts melted when he met the risen Saviour. He had been absent the first time Jesus had appeared to His band of disciples, but the next time Thomas was with them.

Tenderly, Jesus invited Thomas to do what he had said he must do before he would believe: "Reach hither thy finger, and behold my hands; and reach hither thy hand, and thrust it into my side; and be not faithless, but believing" (John 20:27).

It wasn't necessary. Thomas had seen enough. He cried out in adoring worship, "My Lord and my God" (John 20:28).

A fresh vision of Jesus does wonders for us when we are struggling with doubt. Unlike Thomas' experience, ours does not come through physical contact with the Saviour but by the Holy Spirit's revelation of Him.

If bad circumstances are an excuse for doubt, no one had a better excuse than Paul. But he did not fall into this trap. No one ever kept his spiritual equilibrium in the midst of trouble like this man. In 2 Corinthians 4:8,9 he wrote: "We are troubled on every side, yet not distressed; we are perplexed, but not in despair; persecuted, but not forsaken; cast down, but not destroyed."

Was Paul superhuman? No, he was a mortal like the rest of us. But he had grasped the secret of victory in every situation. "We walk by faith, not by sight" (2 Corinthians 5:7). "Sight" told Paul everything was against him and he was headed for disaster. But faith assured Paul that through his trials Jesus Christ was being revealed to the world (2 Corinthians 4:10).

One of the worst things doubt can produce is self-pity. We cannot afford to indulge in it, and Paul didn't. He considered his trials simply an opportunity to share in the sufferings of Christ (2 Corinthians 1:5). Paul was not surprised or discouraged by trials when they struck; he kept on top of them because he walked by faith.

Doubt Is Deadly

We should pay close attention to any areas of doubt that distract us from the walk of faith. We may have to limit or even eliminate our association with people who constantly express doubt. Drastic changes in our own thinking may be necessary. This is not accomplished by clenching our fists and saying, "From now on I'm not entertaining any negative, defeatist thoughts." We must simply fill our hearts and minds so full of God's Word that no room is left for doubt.

Defeating doubt is worth any effort it takes to do it. Unchecked, doubt can have serious effects on our relationship with the Lord. Doubt can turn into cynicism or actual unbelief. This will cause our ministry of encouragement to others and the joy in our hearts to diminish. What kind of testimony would this be to the gospel of Christ we profess to believe?

We are not struggling alone in our efforts to overcome doubt. The Holy Spirit is our Helper. The Word of God can bring new life to our flagging spirits. God, our heavenly Father, is concerned about us and daily stretches out His helping hand. He intends for us to win the battle, not lose it.

Never forget Jesus' promise:

> Verily I say unto you, If ye have faith, and doubt not, ye shall not only do this which is done to the fig tree, but also if ye shall say unto this mountain, Be thou removed, and be thou cast into the sea; it shall be done. And all things, whatsoever ye shall ask in prayer, believing, ye shall receive (Matthew 21:21,22).

7

Everyone Feels It Sometime

READ 1 KINGS 19; PSALM 27

Loneliness is real, and it hurts. But it can be dealt with victoriously and actually serve to help us mature spiritually. Above all, it can enable us to extend a helping hand to others. If we never felt lonely, we would have a hard time understanding those who do.

Loneliness is a normal human reaction to certain conditions. It is neither a sin nor a cause for having guilty feelings.

It is part of our human makeup to become adjusted to our environment and to some extent depend on it for emotional support. One of the most common causes of loneliness is the removal of some strong supporting element from that environment. The separation may be temporary or permanent. It may be caused by moving, divorce, or death. When we are fatigued or sick, the loneliness is compounded. Our physical condition magnifies the emotional loss, and the combination can be overwhelming.

Does the Bible say anything about loneliness? Indeed it does. The Bible contains a number of accounts of believers tormented by loneliness.

A Case Study

Some of Elijah's experiences make a classic case study of loneliness. Watching that rugged prophet in the beginning of his ministry, we would never suspect that later we would see him despondent and lonely. But it happened.

First Kings 18 records the dramatic confrontation between Elijah and the prophets of Baal. When God answered by fire, the issue was settled about who was really God. Baal's prophets were executed.

However, chapter 19 finds Elijah in a completely different setting. Wicked Queen Jezebel heard of the defeat and slaughter of her prophets and swore revenge. Elijah left the scene fast.

At the end of the first day of his flight, the prophet sank exhausted to the ground under a juniper tree. Bone-deep weariness engulfed him and he fell asleep—but not before he had prayed to die.

The Lord sent an angel with food and words of encouragement, and Elijah finally got up and spent the next 40 days traveling to Mount Horeb (*i.e.*, Mt. Sinai). There he found a cave where the darkness matched his own feelings.

But God was monitoring His tired, depressed servant and finally got his attention. "What are you doing here, Elijah?" the Lord asked. Elijah informed God that he was the only one left holding up the banner of righteousness. Furthermore Elijah declared, he was in mortal danger because of his courageous stand.

"I, even I only, am left." The words reflected the heavy feeling of loneliness that had wrapped itself around Elijah's spirit (1 Kings 19:10). Nothing depresses us more than to champion a cause and feel that everyone has deserted us.

But everyone *hadn't* deserted. Elijah *wasn't* the only righteous one left. In "a still small voice" God spoke to the once fiery but now overwrought prophet. He told him of 7,000 Israelites who had not bowed to Jezebel's false god (1 Kings 19:12-18).

At the same time God gave Elijah a new task. He was to find Elisha and anoint him as his successor in the prophetic office. He was also commissioned to anoint a new king of Israel.

Elijah obeyed, and his depression seemed to lift quickly. He became involved in the Lord's work again instead of allowing his thoughts to depress him. He was cheered by the knowledge that many others were still serving the Lord. Things were not as bad as his tortured emotions had led him to think.

David Too

Usually we think of David singing psalms as he sat on the hillside watching his sheep. But several of those psalms tell us that he sometimes traveled a road of loneliness.

Psalm 27 is an example. In verse 9 David cries to the Lord, "Leave me not, neither forsake me, O God of my salvation." Others had forsaken him, and in his distress the thought apparently occurred to him that God might do the same. He quickly received assurance, however, that this would not happen. In the next verse David writes: "When my father and my mother forsake me, then the Lord will take me up."

Psalm 142 records an experience which was so agonizing to David that he says his spirit was "overwhelmed" (v. 3). Human help had vanished and David cried, "Refuge failed me; no man cared for my soul" (v. 4).

At that time David's life was in danger. He was running from King Saul and hiding in a cave. He had companions who had joined his cause, yet he felt he was all alone and no one cared.

In both of these psalms David emerges with a new vision of his God. In Psalm 27:11 he prays, "Teach me thy way, O Lord, and lead me in a plain path, because of mine enemies." In Psalm 142:5 he writes: "I cried unto thee, O Lord: I said, Thou art my refuge and my portion in the land of the living."

A Lonely Wrestling Match

Jacob was experiencing difficulties he had brought on himself. He had to flee for his life after cheating his brother Esau out of the family birthright. He knew he could not run forever, and someday he must meet Esau again.

In Genesis 32 we find Jacob on his way to keep that rendezvous. He had gone to a lonely spot to grapple with his fears and frustrations. We read in verse 24: "And Jacob was left alone."

But Jacob soon discovered he was not alone after all. A supernatural being appeared—undoubtedly an angel in some kind of human form. The two began to wrestle. The real struggle was inside Jacob. Victory did not come until Jacob surrendered to the one who had come as God's representative.

When it was all over, Jacob had secured a new name, Israel, and a new relationship with the Lord. Such an outcome made the struggles of those lonely hours worthwhile.

Jesus Understands

Hebrews 5:15 assures us that Jesus was tested "in all points" like we are. This included the test of loneliness He went through in the beginning of His ministry during His temptation.

He was in the loneliest of all lonely places—a barren desert. Mark adds the detail that He "was with the wild beasts" (Mark 1:13). What company! Their mournful howls would add to any feelings of desolation. Forty days of going without food had left Jesus hungry and exhausted.

No human companions were at His side when Satan struck with all his fury. Yet Jesus drove the enemy back again and again with the sword of the Spirit, the Word of God. Finally Satan retreated and angels came to minister to God's Son (Matthew 4:11).

When it was all over, "Jesus returned in the power of the Spirit into Galilee" (Luke 4:14). The lonely days did not destroy Him. He was strengthened by the experience. Now He would begin His glorious earthly ministry.

Then 3 years later came the final hours. We see the human side of Jesus as He asked three of His disciples to accompany Him to the area of the Garden where He was going to pray. He couldn't take them all the way, for it was a conflict that He must engage in by himself. But He wanted the support and companionship of those men with whom He had been so closely associated.

What a disappointment it was to Jesus when Peter, James, and John kept falling asleep. If you have trusted a friend who let you down when you needed him most, our Saviour understands. He had that kind of experience that night in the Garden.

Yet Jesus came out of the battle victorious. He had submitted to the Father's will with the prayer, "Not as I will, but as thou wilt" (Matthew 26:39). Before He left the place of prayer, an angel came to His side to strengthen Him (Luke 22:43). He had prayed alone, but He had not been forsaken, and neither are you and I—ever.

Jesus' loneliness had not yet reached its fiercest moment. It was on the cross where it became so intense that He cried in agony, "My God, my God, why hast thou forsaken me?" (Matthew 27:46). We have a Saviour who understands, for He was lonely himself.

Eleven Lonely Men

No one ever felt more lonely than Jesus' band of disciples during the last few hours before His death. Judas had left to complete his scheme to betray Jesus, and the Twelve were now the Eleven. After eating the Last Supper they had left the Upper Room in an atmosphere of heaviness.

Jesus would not have any more opportunities to talk with these men before His ordeal of suffering. So He used those precious hours to bring His disciples words of comfort.

The most important truth Jesus brought to the sorrowing group was that although He was leaving, they would not be alone. "I will not leave you comfortless," He promised (John 14:18). The word "comfortless" means "orphans." They were not going to be spiritual orphans. The Holy Spirit was coming from heaven to stand in Jesus' place. Jesus called the Spirit the Comforter.

When the Spirit came at Pentecost, the disciples realized they were not alone even though Jesus was no longer physically present. The Holy Spirit made the Saviour real to them and brought them strength and courage. The same Spirit ministers to us as we follow Jesus.

Paul in the Storm

In Acts 27:13-25 the apostle Paul was on board a ship taking him to Rome for trial. Most of the company on board were ungodly people, so their presence was no consolation. Can we doubt that the apostle spent some lonely hours? To make matters worse, a terrible storm moved in, and everyone was afraid they were going to the bottom of the sea. What intensifies lonely feelings more than dark clouds and stormy weather?

Then something happened to reassure Paul he was not alone. God sent an angel to his side during the night with the message, "Fear not, Paul" (v. 24). No life was going to be lost—the Lord promised. Besides having his own spirits lifted, Paul was able to encourage the others: "Wherefore, sirs, be of good cheer: for I believe God, that it shall be even as it was told me" (v. 25).

When we come to the end of Paul's second letter to Timothy we can certainly sense a feeling of loneliness in the apostle's heart. He was in prison, awaiting execution. His companions had left, including a trusted helper, Demas, who had decided the world had more to offer than Christ (2 Timothy 4:10).

"Only Luke is with me," wrote Paul. Before closing the letter, Paul told of a time when "all men forsook me" (v. 16). But he added: "Notwithstanding the Lord stood with me, and strengthened me. . . . And the Lord shall deliver me from every evil work, and will preserve me unto his heavenly kingdom" (vv. 17,18). Even as his life drew to a close, Paul knew he was not alone.

In the Spirit

The apostle John was exiled to the Isle of Patmos for the crime of preaching the gospel. From what we know of that island, a more desolate spot for a prisoner could not have been selected.

Yet, while he was in those bleak surroundings, John wrote the Book of Revelation. He describes how it happened: "I was in the Spirit on the Lord's day" (Revelation 1:10).

On a barren island, but in the Spirit—what victory! If loneliness had been in John's heart, it took flight when the Spirit quickened his faith and spiritual perception.

That John had his lonely days and nights seems a safe

assumption. But on that particular day, something wonderful happened. The Spirit of God swept over the dreariness of that island prison and showed John that God, not Caesar, was in control.

God is still in control; He always will be. One element of loneliness is the feeling that somehow the situation is out of hand. We have lost our grip on things and no way exists to get hold of them again. Raw nerves and a tired mind send us all kinds of wrong signals.

God has made us social creatures and we need the company of others. Some people make the mistake, however, of gearing their lives to constant activity and crowds, with little time for solitude. This kind of schedule eventually brings one to the place where he cannot stand to be alone at all.

We will fortify ourselves best in coping with loneliness if we are not so dependent on company that its absence knocks the props out from under us. Above all, we need regular, unhurried times of solitude with God. "Be still, and know that I am God" (Psalm 46:10) may be one of the most overlooked verses in the Bible. Surely John on the Isle of Patmos must have thought of it.

How about Isaiah 30:15: "In quietness and in confidence shall be your strength." Some people are ready to climb the walls if they suddenly find things quiet.

Jesus said it so well just before He went to the cross: "Ye . . . shall leave me alone: and yet I am not alone, because the Father is with me" (John 16:32). Alone, yet not alone. Being deprived of human company doesn't have to be synonymous with loneliness, and it won't be if we earnestly cultivate our fellowship with God.

8

An Empty Stomach Hurts

READ GENESIS 3:14-19; MATTHEW 6:24-34; 1 JOHN
3:16,17

Since God created the world why are so many people
going hungry? Does He intend for me to do anything
about it?

If sin had not entered the world, we would have none
of the ills that plague the human race. There would be
no death, sickness, pain, crime, or war—and no hunger.

On the third day of creation, among the things God
made was " 'all kinds of plants, those that bear grain and
those that bear fruit' " (Genesis 1:11, *Good News Bible*).

After creating man, God said to him, " 'I have provided
all kinds of grain and all kinds of fruit for you to eat' "
(Genesis 1:29, *Good News Bible*). In the next verse God
told Adam that He had provided food for all the birds
and animals.

We are awed to realize that our gigantic universe was
created by a word from God. But is it not inspiring to
note that the same Creator was concerned that both
humans and animals have an adequate food supply?

Genesis 2 is a detailed review of God's work of creation. We read in verse 8 that "the Lord God planted a
garden eastward in Eden; and there he put the man
whom he had formed." Think of it—God planting a gar-

den. He wanted man to have a beautiful and enjoyable environment.

In verse 9 we are told: "Out of the ground made the Lord God to grow every tree that is pleasant to the sight, and good for food." Furthermore, God provided a perfect irrigation system for the vegetation that would provide His creatures' food: "A river went out of Eden to water the garden" (Genesis 2:10). There would be no crop failures because of drought.

Adam was not going to loll in the sun and do nothing. God assigned him what some would consider a most enjoyable task: "The Lord God took the man, and put him into the garden of Eden to dress it and to keep it" (Genesis 2:15).

The Beautiful Scene Spoiled

In the first two chapters of Genesis we have a picture of the world as God intended it. Obviously it is not that way today, and the Bible tells us how that beautiful scene was spoiled.

It was necessary that God make man a free moral agent, not a robot. Of course this was a risk, and God knew what would happen. But He could not have enjoyed fellowship with a creature who had no power of choice.

Man exercised his power of choice and disobeyed his Maker. The consequences of this rebellion affected the whole world. Besides the curse that fell on humans, the peace of the animal creation was disturbed. Paul describes it like this: "For we know that the whole creation groaneth and travaileth in pain together until now" (Romans 8:22).

Now we come to the part of the curse that helps us understand why the world has crop failures, food shortages, and famines. Still addressing Adam, God declared:

Cursed is the ground for thy sake; in sorrow shalt thou eat of it all the days of thy life; thorns also and thistles shall it bring forth to thee; and thou shalt eat the herb of the field: in the sweat of thy face shalt thou eat bread, till thou return unto the ground (Genesis 3:17-19).

Several chapters later we read of a famine. It was so "grievous" that Abraham left the Promised Land and went to Egypt (Genesis 12:10).

As the population has increased and man has interfered more and more with the environment, famine has become so prevalent that it is a way of life in many parts of the world today. Jesus said that famines would be one of the signs of the end of this age (Matthew 24:7).

When Jesus returns and lifts the curse, one of the great changes will be the elimination of famine. Amos 9:13 is a beautiful prophecy of that coming day:

" 'The days are coming,' says the Lord, 'when grain will grow faster than it can be harvested, and grapes will grow faster than the wine can be made. The mountains will drip with sweet wine, and the hills will flow with it' " *(Good News Bible)*.

Isaiah saw the same glorious day of liberation: "The wilderness and the solitary place shall be glad for them; and the desert shall rejoice, and blossom as the rose" (Isaiah 35:1).

But the Millennium Isn't Here Yet

Until God shifts the calendar into the millennial era, famine will continue to plague mankind. We hear much about energy shortages, but those who are trying to plan for the future also envision a dire food shortage that may affect even affluent nations. Some have proposed a world food bank to try to avert such a crisis or at least lessen its impact.

Obviously, prevention is better than cure where famine is concerned. Christian professionals are needed in the front lines of research, production, processing, and food distribution. Ways must be found to maintain a better balance of nature to maximize food production and distribution.

Christians with expertise in the field of agriculture who feel called to help backward nations improve their farming methods can consider their work a true ministry.

God's Intervening Mercy

The Bible does not record every famine that has occurred, but it does mention 13 of them. Most of these came as a judgment from God.

Yet God always tempers judgment with mercy. Despite the curse, God has often intervened miraculously to spare people the full consequences of sin's devastation. An outstanding example is His provision during the Egyptian famine of Joseph's time.

Before the terrible years of crop failure in Egypt, God blessed the land with 7 years of bumper crops. Through a dream God gave Pharaoh (and interpreted through Joseph), the Egyptians were warned and able to prepare for the bad years. Thus they averted what surely would have been widespread starvation (Genesis 41:1-44).

David testified: "I have been young, and now am old; yet have I not seen the righteous forsaken, nor his seed begging bread" (Psalm 37:25).

One of the spectacular demonstrations of God's loving care was His preservation of Elijah during the 3-year drought and subsequent famine which God sent as judgment during Ahab's reign (1 Kings 17:2-16).

Jesus looked at the effortless way birds are provided with food. He observed that they do not sow, reap, or gather food like people do. Yet the fowls of the air are well nourished. Then He pointed out that human life is much more valuable.

Jesus appealed to believers to look to God for their daily provision as an antidote to anxiety and worry. He was not implying that they should become lazy or unproductive. He was saying, in effect, "Don't worry; don't be anxious. Don't neglect your spiritual nature for physical or material things." In other words, don't make survival the primary motive for living. Use your spiritual resources in maintaining a balanced life (see Matthew 6:24-34).

When Jesus gave the disciples a pattern for their prayer life, one of the petitions He encouraged was, "Give us this day our daily bread" (Matthew 6:11). This refers not only to food, but to all of our material needs. Would our Saviour have told us to pray this way if our Heavenly Father were not concerned about our being clothed and fed? Of course not.

The Early Church Pointed the Way

The Early Church recognized the responsibility of caring for its members who were unable to provide for their own needs. Acts 6 describes one of the problems that arose in the beginning.

The massive task of feeding members of the church from a common storehouse was complicated by the church's rapid growth. Friction between the two major language groups led to discontent. The Greek-speaking members complained that their widows were being shortchanged when supplies were distributed. They charged that the Hebrew-speaking widows were being favored.

The task of food distribution had become too large for the apostles to handle if they were to continue their vital spiritual leadership. Yet they were not willing to neglect the work, for they recognized that the responsibility of feeding these people could not be shirked.

In order to handle the work more efficiently and fairly, the church chose seven men to assume the responsibility. They did their job so well that the tension subsided immediately and the spiritual revival continued.

Persecution of Christians in Jerusalem drove many of them from their homes. Many fled to Antioch in the north. During the visit of some of the church's leaders to Antioch, the Holy Spirit prompted Agabus to prophesy that a severe famine was coming (Acts 11:28). The Antioch believers knew this would create special hardships for the Jerusalem church. They quickly received an offering to send to their brethren in the capital city.

The New Testament sets a pattern for churches of all time to follow in taking care of their own members. Even though government agencies have been formed and social programs exist, material ministry to the needy of a congregation is still a vital part of Christian stewardship.

Individual Responsibility

Paul continually emphasized that salvation is by grace, "not of works, lest any man should boast" (Ephesians 2:9). Nevertheless, he made it clear that Christians are "created in Christ Jesus to do good works" (Ephesians 2:10, NIV). James was also concerned that even though we are saved by grace we should be careful to demonstrate our faith by good works. Part of our good works concerns those with physical and material needs.

> What good is it, my brothers, if a man claims to have faith but has no deeds? Can such faith save him? Suppose a brother or sister is without clothes and daily food. If one of

you says to him, "Go, I wish you well; keep warm and well fed," but does nothing about his physical needs, what good is it? (James 2:14-16, NIV).

John emphasized the same theme:

Hereby perceive we the love of God, because he laid down his life for us: and we ought to lay down our lives for the brethren. But whoso hath this world's good, and seeth his brother have need, and shutteth up his bowels of compassion from him, how dwelleth the love of God in him? My little children, let us not love in word, neither in tongue; but in deed and in truth (1 John 3:16-18).

Both James and John were teaching that practical Christianity involves a ministry to the physical needs of fellow Christians while rejoicing with them in their salvation. What is the value, these Early Church leaders asked, if a person has tremendous faith in God but does nothing about the plight of a brother or sister lacking clothing or food?

John adds an emotional element to Christian benevolence. He speaks of having "no pity" (NIV). Meeting the bodily needs of other Christians should be more than a cold financial transaction. It must spring out of love. If the love of God dwells in the Christian, John declares, then his emotions must be involved in Christian stewardship. So, he concludes, don't just talk about love. Demonstrate it.

The Job Will Never End

It is encouraging that many churches and Christian organizations are in the forefront of efforts today to relieve the hunger that has overtaken so much of the world. It is not a task that will last a year or two, but until Jesus returns.

Although we hear of the hunger problem often, we must guard against becoming indifferent. Putting ourselves in the shoes of others is not easy. When we never have an empty stomach, imagining how hunger feels is difficult. We must make a prayerful effort to keep our hearts sensitive to the millions who are actually dying for lack of food.

God has blessed our own land above all others on earth. We could feed thousands—and possibly millions—with the food we *waste*. Has God granted America such abundance for lavishing on herself? Or does He intend that we should lead the way in ministering to the starving millions around the world?

We are grateful for the secular organizations that are doing so much to alleviate the misery of world hunger. But we must avoid the temptation to imagine that their efforts relieve the Church of its obligations. Never will enough people be working at this gigantic task. The financial needs to carry it out are enormous and will continue to grow. But in spite of this and inflation we are still financially blessed; we must not fail to be good stewards of the material wealth God has entrusted to us.

At the judgment Jesus will commend those who have ministered to the hungry, thirsty, lonely, ill-dressed, sick, and imprisoned (Matthew 25:35,36). The Saviour's view of these benevolent acts is: "Inasmuch as ye have done it unto one of the least of these my brethren, ye have done it unto me" (Matthew 25:40).

9

Be Careful! It's a Trap!

READ DEUTERONOMY 18:10-14; 1 CHRONICLES
10:13,14; ACTS 8:9-13

What's wrong with a little fortune-telling and astrology? It's just innocent fun—or is it?

Man is a creature of great curiosity. Sometimes this has led to inventions and great discoveries that have benefited the human race.

But curiosity can also be dangerous, even fatal. The kind we are looking at in this study should be avoided.

Practice of the black arts has a long history. Today we often classify this kind of activity under the term *occult*. *The World Book Encyclopedia* defines "occult" this way:

> Occult is a term which refers to knowledge of a supernatural type, not bounded by the strict laws of modern science. A person may be said to have knowledge of the occult if he claims to understand subjects which cannot be understood by ordinary men, and which are outside the field of recognized science.

"Occult" means secret, or mysterious. Revivals of occultism have occurred from time to time in all parts of the world. Some aspects of it have persisted through the centuries, particularly astrology, fortune-telling, and spiritism (necromancy, or communing with the dead).

The explosion of interest in occult practices in our own day is a phenomenon. Probably it has happened because the times we live in are so troubled and uncertain.

False Promises

All occult practices involve basically the same assurances to adherents: they can know the future; they can tap hidden powers that will give them better control over their lives. Occultism appears to offer a sense of security through information hidden to outsiders.

All of these false promises are contained in the modern occultic practices of astrology, transcendental meditation, witchcraft, fortune-telling, Ouija boards, tarot cards, and related activities.

Why should children of the Lord seek knowledge about the future in these forbidden areas? Jesus taught that the Christian need not be caught up in predicting what lies ahead. The Father knows the "times before appointed" (see Matthew 24:36; Acts 17:26); that should be adequate security for His children.

Resting in the knowledge of God's loving concern for each individual, the Christian is admonished in the Bible to get on with the business of living and witnessing. Reliance on God allows the believer to approach each of life's crises as an opportunity to be led by the Holy Spirit.

To be caught up in predicting the future is to avoid the opportunity to use the present time wisely. For that reason, the Christian has no need to consult fortune-tellers, mediums, horoscopes, Ouija boards, or tarot cards. They are an abomination to the Lord. Innocent as some of these activities appear to be, anyone dabbling with them is flirting with the devil.

Here's What God Says

In many respects occultism seeks to counterfeit the true religion of Jesus Christ. This is what makes it so deadly; many people cannot tell the false from the true.

The interest Americans have today in Eastern religions is amazing. How strange that people will turn away from the peace God gives through Christ and yet spend so much time and energy reaching for the false, deceptive peace offered by these philosophies from the East.

Beginning in the Old Testament the Bible is full of warnings about the occult. This shows us how ancient and deep-rooted this evil is. God has declared himself on the subject, leaving no doubt about where He stands on the issue of the occult.

Some areas of the occult today are anti-God. How widespread the worship of Satan has become is difficult to know, but it is prevalent enough to be frightening. Other occult teaching is more subtle, sophisticated.

In the land of Canaan the Israelites found people who had been enslaved by occultism for centuries. The idols they worshiped were simply outward symbols of the invisible demons behind them. Consequently, God warned His people sternly about these insidious practices:

> There shall not be found among you any one that maketh his son or his daughter to pass through the fire, or that useth divination, or an observer of times, or an enchanter, or a witch, or a charmer, or a consulter with familiar spirits, or a wizard, or a necromancer. For all that do these things are an abomination unto the Lord: and because of these abominations the Lord thy God doth drive them out from before thee (Deuteronomy 18:10-12).

A King and a Witch

One of the most striking Old Testament accounts of the tragedy of occultism concerns King Saul. Having lost touch with God through his arrogance and disobedience, and being faced by the armies of the Philistines, Saul turned to a spiritist medium (1 Samuel 28).

Previously Saul had conducted a campaign against those who practiced black magic; now he was seeking help from the occult himself. Disguising himself so he would not be recognized as the king, Saul went by night to a witch in the village of Endor.

God upset the séance. The witch (literally "a woman controlling, or mistress of a divining demon") was trying to communicate with her familiar spirit, but instead she actually saw Samuel. She screamed in fright, for she had not expected the dead prophet to appear.

Furthermore, Samuel spoke directly to Saul, and not through the medium. His words to the king were a pronouncement of coming doom. The medium had not brought Samuel back from the other side. God had sent him, completely confounding the witch and demoralizing Saul.

Turning to a medium who consulted with familiar spirits was Saul's final act of disobedience to God. It led to his death the following day (1 Chronicles 10:13,14). Dabbling in the occult was fatal to the man who had been anointed king of his nation.

The Gospel Versus the Occult

Acts 8 records a great revival in Samaria under Philip's ministry. An interesting fact is injected into the account:

> There was a certain man, called Simon, which beforetime in the same city used sorcery, and bewitched the people of Samaria, giving out that himself was some great one: To whom they all gave heed, from the least to the greatest, saying, This man is the great power of God. And to him they had regard, because that of long time he had bewitched them with sorceries (Acts 8:9-11).

The sorcerer soon lost his grip on the Samaritans. Multitudes, responding to the gospel, were saved and healed. Demons were cast out. When Peter and John came from Jerusalem to pray for the new converts, they were filled with the Holy Spirit.

Simon was dumbfounded, and he sought to buy the power to impart the Holy Spirit to people. Peter's reply to Simon's request was a blistering indictment and a blunt warning. The last we hear of the sorcerer, he is imploring Peter to pray that the things spoken of him will not happen (Acts 8:18-24).

The devastation of the power of the occult in Samaria through the preaching of the gospel is a glorious testimony. Only eternity will reveal the multitudes delivered from the slavery of the occult by turning to Christ.

Paul and Barnabas were commissioned by the Holy Spirit for special missionary work. Shortly thereafter they encountered the occult. A Roman official named Sergius Paulus was eager to hear the gospel and called for the two preachers. A sorcerer who had gained influence with the official was alarmed when it appeared he might be put out of his position.

When Paul and Barnabas tried to preach, Elymas the sorcerer immediately withstood them. The evil man did everything in his power to persuade Sergius Paulus not to listen.

Filled with the Holy Spirit, Paul rebuked the sorcerer, who was then temporarily blinded by the judgment of God. He had to be led about by others. As a result of this display of God's power, Sergius Paulus accepted Christ. Again the gospel had triumphed over Satan's work (Acts 13:4-12).

Satan Doesn't Give Up Easily

Paul and Silas encountered the occult again at Philippi

77

(Acts 16:16-34). As they went about their ministry they were continually followed by a demon-possessed girl. By the power of Satan she seemed to possess the ability to foretell the future. The wicked men who controlled her were making a handsome profit from her work.

After the young woman had followed and harassed Paul and Silas many days, Paul cast the demon out of her. Immediately her fortune-telling powers were gone, and so was the money she could make for her masters. Her owners were so furious they succeeded in having Paul and Silas jailed.

God shook the jail with an earthquake that night, and the warden and his family were converted. What a victory for the name of Jesus! Once more the power of Satan—manifesting itself through the power of the occult—had been swept aside.

Again in Ephesus the gospel and the occult clashed, and again the gospel smashed the devil's powers:

> And many that believed came, and confessed, and showed their deeds. Many of them also which used curious arts brought their books together, and burned them before all men: and they counted the price of them, and found it fifty thousand pieces of silver. So mightily grew the word of God and prevailed (Acts 19:18-20).

Paul warned Timothy that "in the latter times some shall depart from the faith, giving heed to seducing spirits, and doctrines of devils" (1 Timothy 4:1).

We are warned in the Word to "believe not every spirit, but try the spirits whether they are of God" (1 John 4:1). This power to discern the spirits is a part of the Holy Spirit's operation in the lives of believers. It comes as a gift of the Spirit and is functional for those who seek to be led by Him.

Occult practices will intensify near the end of this age

and will be one of Satan's methods of enslaving multitudes. Despite the divine judgments poured out on earth during the Great Tribulation, we read in Revelation 9:21 of an astounding reaction of the wicked: "Neither repented they of their murders, nor of their sorceries, nor of their fornication, nor of their thefts." Note here how sorcery is included with murder, sexual immorality, and theft. Dabbling in the occult breaks down an individual's resistance to every other sin; it opens the door for Satan to take over the whole life.

In Revelation 18:23, the angel charged with executing judgment on Babylon cries, "For thy merchants were the great men of the earth; for by thy sorceries were all nations deceived."

Note the widespread influence of Babylon's sorceries. "All nations" are affected.

No Occultists in Heaven

One of the most striking passages concerning the fate of the wicked is found in Revelation 21:8. Again we are impressed with the company in which occultists are included:

> But the fearful, and unbelieving, and the abominable, and murderers, and whoremongers, and *sorcerers,* and idolaters, and all liars, shall have their part in the lake which burneth with fire and brimstone: which is the second death (italics added).

As if to sound a final warning concerning the occult, the Bible lists in Revelation those who are forever excluded from heaven: ". . . dogs, and *sorcerers,* and whoremongers, and murderers, and idolaters, and whosoever loveth and maketh a lie" (Revelation 22:15; italics added).

Satan has many traps, but the occult is one of the

deadliest. People who have a religious inclination but lack adequate Bible knowledge are often an easy prey. Occultists may sometimes invoke the name of Jesus in an attempt to show the respectability of their teaching. Spiritists have even referred to Jesus as a highly skilled medium. But the only contact with the spirit world that the Bible endorses is contact with God, contact made through prayer.

Nevertheless, there are spirits in the universe opposed to God. As spirit beings, they are invisible and operate above natural laws. They use their superhuman knowledge to function through spiritist mediums, fortune-tellers, and others who make themselves Satan's tools.

At the same time, some who engage in these activities are plain fakes, having no real powers. Even so we dare not risk exposing ourselves to the enemy of our souls by experimentation, no matter how innocent the circumstances.

Although we are living in dangerous, deceptive times and anyone would be imprudent to flirt with the enemy, a child of God need not cringe in fear of his power. "Greater is he that is in you, than he that is in the world" (1 John 4:4).

10

Home, Sweet Home

READ EPHESIANS 5:21 THROUGH 6:4

In recent years we have witnessed a shattering of old values concerning the home. Have we been mistaken in our past beliefs? Is respect for parents really important? What about fidelity between husband and wife? Do parents owe their children any more than board, room, and laundry? Must they be concerned about teaching their children moral values and giving them spiritual training? Isn't that the church's responsibility?

A High Honor

God intended that marriage point to a higher, eternal relationship, the relationship between Christ and the Church. Husbands have the high honor of representing Christ in marriage. Wives have the high honor of representing the Church.

The New Testament does not teach that women are inferior to men, for Paul wrote: "There is neither male nor female: for ye are all one in Christ" (Galatians 3:28). But in the organizational structure of the home, the Lord has ordained the husband to be the primary decision-maker. If he obeys the Biblical command to love his wife, her needs and desires will obviously influence the decisions he makes.

81

The teaching that a wife must be in submission to her husband is found in other parts of the New Testament also (Colossians 3:18; Titus 2:5; 1 Peter 3:1-6). But nowhere does the reason for submission receive such emphasis as in the following passage: "Therefore as the church is subject unto Christ, so let the wives be to their own husbands in every thing" (Ephesians 5:24).

Much of the furor today about the wife's submission arises from a misunderstanding or rejection of the Bible's teaching. Some have attempted to build their case by arousing emotions about the wife's "rights," implying that the traditional role demeans her.

We cannot base our beliefs on this kind of distorted thinking. The Bible is the only marriage guide that is totally reliable. Too many writers and speakers allow their own prejudices to influence the information they dispense. Rather than the Biblical concept putting the wife down, it exalts her.

Note the principle underscored in Ephesians 5:23: "For the husband is the head of the wife, even as Christ is the head of the church: and he is the saviour of the body."

As the Church's Saviour, Christ watches over every member of the Church with never-ceasing care. He protects the Church from its enemies. Christ is both Head and Saviour, and Paul declares this pictures the husband's position in marriage. He is the head of the family, but he is also its protector and provider. He is concerned every waking moment with the welfare of his wife and all the family.

When humans try to disrupt this Biblical arrangement they create the same chaos in the home as rebellious Christians cause when they refuse to be submissive to Christ.

Subjection is a word that often provokes people's feelings. This is especially true since the emergence of all the movements that emphasize "rights." Promoters of such causes sometimes fail to realize that without submission there is no social order.

In the processes of education, business, government—at whatever level—decisionmaking roles must exist. Even in the sports world somebody has to coach. And teams call for captains. Imagine a football game in which the coach's instructions are ignored and it's every player for himself.

Marriage will be enriched, not hindered, when a couple live their lives according to the Biblical example, instead of the world's ideas about submission.

Back to the Beginning

The relationship between husband and wife goes back to the beginning of the human race. When God created the first couple and brought them together He declared they were one flesh. For this reason their commitment to each other takes precedence over every other human relationship (Genesis 2:24). Jesus sanctioned and reemphasized this truth, adding the solemn admonition, "What therefore God hath joined together, let not man put asunder" (Matthew 19:6).

Clearly, God's marriage plan is one man for one woman for life. Flirtations, extramarital affairs—anything that stains the fidelity of either partner—cannot be condoned. They are out of the question if marital integrity is to be preserved.

There is no such thing as an innocent flirtation. Any spouse who tries such an experiment toys with tragedy. For although he or she will bear the responsibility of such irresponsible behavior, marriage and family will share the consequences.

According to the Bible, marriage is a permanent commitment. The Scriptures allow no trial marriages, no live-in arrangements that can be discontinued at the whim of either partner. The marriage license is not a mere scrap of paper, and the wedding ceremony is not an outdated relic to be scorned by so-called moderns. Rather, they are a vital part of a sacred commitment by two people to each other. It is a commitment so significant that the couple is glad for the whole world to know about it. How appropriate for the ceremony to be marked by Scripture reading and the invoking of God's blessings on the union.

People who have no comprehension of the Bible's eternal principles will laugh, "We're living in the 20th century. Nobody pays any attention to those old ideas anymore." But God's Word stands firm and unchanging. If we are interested in completeness, in being whole persons, and in having whole marriages, we will abide by God's rules. We will pay dearly if we do not. We cannot break God's laws without suffering the consequences.

God created man first. He created woman because man was not complete by himself. Some of the most beautiful words in the creation account are found in Genesis 2:18: "The Lord God said, It is not good that the man should be alone; I will make him a help meet for him."

The word "meet" is an old one seldom used in this sense anymore. It means suitable. God created a companion whose nature complemented Adam's. Eve was exactly what he needed to make his life complete. Her personality and physical makeup were different from his, but they supplied the characteristics the Creator intentionally omitted when He made man. The creation of woman was not an afterthought. God planned it all the time. For this reason He made man in such a way that he would need woman.

The concepts of unisex and homosexuality are ugly distortions of God's perfect creation. The record is clear: "Male and female created he them" (Genesis 1:27).

Love Is the Key

Paul's picture of marriage is beautifully balanced. He does not talk about submission without quickly emphasizing love: "Husbands, love your wives." But notice the last part of this statememt: ". . . even as Christ also loved the church, and gave himself for it" (Ephesians 5:25). Paul taught that the husband should love his wife as Christ loves the Church. This puts married love on the highest and holiest plane. It eliminates any place for mere lust or animallike behavior.

Who could imagine Christ mistreating, bullying, or battering the Church? His attitude is quite the opposite, for He "gave himself for it." Living and dying, Christ served His bride; He is the husband's example.

Ordinarily a husband will not be called on to die for his wife, but in many ways both large and small, he will exhibit the spirit of loving sacrifice for her. He will gladly do without things he wants—and even needs—if he sees that acquiring them will keep his wife from getting what she must have. He may sometimes cancel personal plans that would preempt an activity very dear to her.

When a husband is like Jesus in love, accepting his leadership is easy for the wife. Being the head of a marriage is not a matter of superiority; it is a matter of responsibility.

Christ's desire for the Church is perfection: "that he might present it to himself a glorious church, not having spot, or wrinkle, or any such thing; but that it should be holy and without blemish" (Ephesians 5:27). Following this great example, a husband should seek to bring out the very best qualities in his wife. He can lift her by his love even as the Lord Jesus lifts us by His love.

One of the ways love is expressed in marriage is through the physical relationship. Someone has said that the basis for a good marriage is high friendship and a pure sex love. Of course, marriage should grow in depth from mere physical attraction to a beautiful inseparable unity on the highest spiritual levels. Only then is God's plan for marriage fully realized. Physical union is but a picture of the unity of the married couple's minds and spirits.

Love That Lasts

Remember the old song, "Believe Me, If All Those Endearing Young Charms"? Did you know that it was first a poem written by Thomas Moore in 1808? While traveling alone, he learned that his wife had been stricken with a disfiguring disease. Here is what he wrote to her:

Believe me, if all those endearing young charms,
Which I gaze on so fondly today,
Were to change by tomorrow, and fleet in my arms,
Like fairy-gifts fading away!
Thou wouldst still be adored, as this moment thou art,
Let thy loveliness fade as it will,
And around the dear ruin each wish of my heart
Would entwine itself verdantly still.

Paul's teaching on marriage in Ephesians 5 ends with these words: ". . . and the wife see that she reverence her husband" (v. 33).

"Reverence" is a word ordinarily associated with one's attitude toward God. Obviously its usage here does not imply a slavish fear accompanied by terror and trembling. Rather, it describes the respect due one from a subordinate. Coupled with the analogy to the relationship between Christ and the Church, such an attitude involves admiration and esteem, courtesy, praise, and the deepest love. How marvelous are marriages that measure up to God's standard.

"One flesh"—what a profound description of the relationship ordained by God for man and wife. The world is suffering today because of widespread disregard of this Biblical concept of marriage.

Home, the First Classroom

Paul tells us that "honor thy father and mother" is "the first commandment with promise" (Ephesians 6:2). The promise connected with this command is "that it may be well with thee, and thou mayest live long on the earth" (Ephesians 6:3). This would indicate that obeying this commandment of God has an effect on one's entire life and even his physical well-being.

Such honor does not stop when we are grown and have our own homes. It extends to the last day our parents are on earth.

The Lord has assigned authority to parents. It is His will that children respect such authority as God-given. A child should be instructed that his parents have more authority in his life than any other person. This includes teachers, coaches, grandparents, other relatives, friends, or neighbors.

Learning obedience to one's parents is the first step in learning to obey God. A child must know that when his parents say to do this, not that, it is an occasion to submit to their will. Just as God makes His will clear to us, parents should make their will clear to their children. To punish a child for something he did not know was against his parents' will is unfair.

Paul gives one reason for obeying parents: It is "right" (Ephesians 6:1). This may not be enough for children with a rebellious nature, but it is the Bible's teaching.

Obeying parents is right because it brings benefit to the child himself. One of the difficult lessons of life is how to cope with authority. Obeying parents is right for the sake of coming generations. Children who obey their parents are more likely to teach proper obedience to their own offspring. A sign of the last days is a universal rejection of the parental leadership (2 Timothy 3:2).

"Honor all people," Peter wrote in 1 Peter 2:17 (New King James Version). This admonition certainly includes parents as objects of respect. As long as they live they are due their children's honor.

Heaven's Little Bundles

If any event calls for a fresh commitment to the will of God for the family it is when wife and husband become mother and father.

It is an incredibly happy moment, but also a sober one.

Children are a gift from God and should be so regarded (Psalm 127:3). They are not nuisances to be tolerated.

Our Heavenly Father is the example parents should follow in their own conduct. The Lord proves His love by disciplining His children (Hebrews 12:5,6).

Listen to Paul's wholesome counsel in Ephesians 6:4: "Fathers, do not exasperate your children; instead, bring them up in the training and instruction of the lord" (NIV). This spiritual responsibility is inescapable. It is a vital part of parenting.

For parents to expect more from their children than their children observe in Mother and Dad is unreasonable. If a parent is careless and indifferent, haphazard, and negligent, the children will likely follow in the same path. On the other hand, the well-ordered life of a parent leaves an indelible impression for good.

11

We're All in This Together

READ 1 CORINTHIANS 12:12-31

How do you size up your role in your church? Some people seem to think of their church as a sort of pleasure bus with comfortable, inactive passengers. But God isn't looking for passengers. He wants participants!

The Holy Spirit used the apostle Paul more than any other Early Church leader to teach us about the function of the Church. First Corinthians 12 is one of the clearest passages on this vital subject.

The Body Is One

First Corinthians 12:12 may sound simple, but it is very basic. "The body is one." The Church has had members in every part of the world. These members have spoken many different languages and lived in varied cultures. Yet in the eyes of God they are members of one Body, the Church.

Verse 13 is not speaking of water baptism or the baptism in the Holy Spirit. Here the Spirit is the Baptizer and the Church is the element into which He baptizes those who are converted. This baptism occurs at the instant of the new birth. At that time the Holy Spirit immerses individuals into the body of Christ. Verse 13 does not refer to the action of joining the membership of any local church or denomination. It is describing the supernatural action of the Holy Spirit. He alone can incorporate people into the true Church, which is Christ's body.

One, But Different

Christians are not to be so much alike that they appear to have all been cut out with the same cookie cutter. Using the human body as an illustration, Paul compares one believer to a hand, another to a foot, one to an eye, another to an ear. How different these parts of the human body are, yet each one is essential to the whole.

God intends that unity should prevail within the body of Christ, yet He does not try to force us all into the same mold. Even in the Early Church one can note great differences in individuals. Peter and Paul were very different in background, training, and personality. Yet God used both of them to accomplish the work He had designated for them.

No Christian should think of himself as any less a part of the Church because his activities seem less important than someone else's. God intends to accomplish a great variety of objectives by means of the Church. He has called and equipped a great variety of people with distinct and different talents so His multiple goals may be realized. One member may feed the hungry, one may visit prisoners, another may minister to the sick, one may care for orphans, and another may teach the illiterate. The list is endless.

The important thing is that each person carry out the purpose God has for him or her within the body of Christ. At the same time, everyone should allow for variety to exist within the Body and not expect all others to fit some kind of preconceived pattern of Christian service.

Mutual Dependence

In every aspect of Christian living each person in the body of Christ is dependent on other members. We tend to take one another for granted until a worker who has been fulfilling his task is removed from the scene. Then we realize how much we benefitted from his almost unnoticed efforts.

The idea of a go-it-alone Christianity surfaces from time to time. "Who needs a church? I can read my Bible and pray without a church or a preacher telling me what to do." So goes the talk of one who fancies himself a rugged individualist.

Such reasoning ignores the basic truth that the Church is God's plan. God expects us to help one another. Much more is expected of a Christian than the selfish goal of personal salvation. To have little regard for other members of the Church is to insult the God who planned that Church even before He created the earth.

First Corinthians 12:18 teaches that God has designated the place for each member of the Body to serve. Verse 20 reflects an underlying principle of the Church's operation in this world: "Many members . . . but one body."

Christians must do more than simply tolerate one another. They must have respect for one another and for the work each one is doing for the Lord.

Perhaps you have noticed someone display the very attitude captured by Paul in his personification of the parts of the human body as saying to one another: "I have no need of thee" (v. 21). This notion is so childish it almost brings a smile; yet we have observed this very attitude in some members of the body of Christ. It not only displeases the Lord, it also hinders the Church's work.

Verses 22-24 set forth some very practical teaching:

> We cannot do without the parts of the body that seem to be weaker; and those parts that we think aren't worth very much are the ones which we treat with greater care; while the parts of the body which don't look very nice are treated with special modesty, which the more beautiful parts do not need. God himself has put the body together in such a way as to give greater honor to those parts that need it *(Good News Bible)*.

The apostle suggests through his analogy that some members of Christ's body are less attractive or less presentable than others. Such people, however, deserve at least as much consideration as we give each of the different parts of our own bodies. God has placed each of us in the body of Christ in close contact with other members so we might benefit, not hurt or hinder, each other.

Mutual Concern

The Lord intends that the members of the Church have a mutual interest and care for one another. We have everything to gain by being part of such an organism. Although I am required to be concerned about the well-being of other members of the Body, my fellow Christians should be equally committed to my best interests.

Pain in the human body illustrates this principle. If the toe steps on a thorn, the whole body is alerted for action. The leg raises the foot to the hand, the eye locates the thorn, the thumb and forefinger grasp it, and the arm and wrist lift it out. A similar cooperative effort should be undertaken by fellow Christians to alleviate the suffering of a member of the body of Christ.

If a person is honored because of a beautiful picture his hands have painted or for winning a race his feet have run, the rest of his body is not jealous. God expects the same mutual admiration and support among the people in the body of Christ when only one of them receives recognition and honor. Jealousy leads to discord and division, and it scars the Body.

"There should be no schism [division] in the body" (1 Corinthians 12:25). That is God's plan for the Church. Harmony does not happen automatically. Every Christian must work at it. Each member will benefit when this ideal is achieved. Everyone will suffer when it is not. God's people are too closely related to be unaffected by the actions and attitudes of one another.

You Are Needed

Although every Christian is a part of the universal Church, that truth is best demonstrated by the Christian's participation in a local church.

Each local congregation can be described as a body; every part (*i.e.*, person) is essential to its effectiveness. Some people have ministries that can be seen: preaching, teaching, singing, playing instruments, etc. Some have behind-the-scenes ministries: intercession, counseling, caring for the sick, etc.

No God-given ministry is unimportant. Every part of the body (*i.e.*, local church) is essential to the well-being of the whole.

Paul lists some of the ministries God has placed in the Church. The list does not attempt to cover every ministry within the Body. It does give an indication, however, of the variety of functions that should be operating within congregations. Above all, the list stresses the participation of many people in the local church if a full range of God-ordained ministries is to be achieved.

Set in the Church

Note Paul's wording in 1 Corinthians 12:28: "God hath set some in the church." The Spirit imparts gifts to individual members so they may function in the Church for the benefit of the whole. The emphasis is on the words "in the church."

The apostles were the leaders of the Early Church, so it is natural for Paul to say, "First apostles." Some insist that *apostle* is a title reserved exclusively for the selected witnesses of Jesus' earthly ministry. Others point out that Paul, although not an eyewitness of Jesus' work, was called an apostle.

In the broadest sense, many are doing the work of an apostle today even though the title appears to be undesirable due to the various interpretations of its meaning. Missionaries who open fields where Christ has never been preached before are certainly doing the work of apostles.

A person used by the Lord in the gift of prophecy is called a prophet. This term does not stress a title; it indicates a function within the local church. A prophet "speaketh unto men to edification, and exhortation, and comfort" (1 Corinthians 14:3). This gift involves spontaneously uttering words given by God in the language of the people for the benefit of assembled believers.

The ministry of teaching cannot be overestimated. Surely pastors are given this ministry, but others may exercise it too. Simply *winning* souls to Christ is not enough. New converts must be trained and nurtured by the ministry of teaching, learning to distinguish, among other things, sound doctrine from false teaching. This is the function as well as the significance of the teacher. He must always be open to the Holy Spirit so that he has the teaching appropriate for the occasion.

A miracle is a supernatural act that contradicts known scientific laws—such as a dead person being restored to life or iron being made to float (2 Kings 4:32-35; 6:5-7). Gifts of healing contradict known scientific laws having to do with the human body. God intervenes with supernatural power that stops the action of diseases and restores health.

One of the least mentioned but indispensable ministries in the Body is called simply "helps." Often those who demonstrate this gift are least aware that they possess it. Yet how quickly the Church would feel the loss if these "gifted" individuals no longer provided their Spirit-anointed helping ministry.

Leadership ability is essential to a smooth-running local church, so the Lord provides some people with the needed gifts ("governments") to get others to work together. Such persons are not greedy for power or recognition, but their gifts of administration will be recognized and utilized by a Spirit-directed church.

In 1 Corinthians 14 Paul makes a distinction between tongues in a public service and tongues in personal devotions. Praying in tongues as a devotional aid is beneficial, Paul declares (vv. 2,4,14,15,17-19). He says, "I would that ye all spake with tongues" (v. 5), no doubt thinking of the devotional value of a God-given prayer language.

But in 1 Corinthians 12:30 Paul asks, "Do all speak with tongues?" The sentence structure implies that the answer is no. This has to do with the public ministry of tongues. Not every believer is to speak out in tongues in public services. Some are selected by the Holy Spirit to provide this ministry. Others are selected by the Spirit to provide interpretation of the utterance in tongues.

When no interpreter is present, speaking in tongues is to be restrained (1 Corinthians 14:27,28). The gift of speaking in tongues—when it functions within Biblical guidelines—is designed to benefit the entire congregation (1 Corinthians 14:5-13,39,40).

Strive to Be Your Best

Every believer should aspire to reach his maximum potential in the Lord. For this reason we should all desire eagerly the higher gifts. These are the gifts that benefit the congregation rather than ourselves as individuals. And once those gifts have been bestowed on us, in their operation we should avoid the competitive, showy manner of the believers at Corinth. Our motivation for the operation of the gifts is to be love—the "more excellent way."

12

Who Wants To Be an Island?

READ MATTHEW 5:38-48; ROMANS 14:7-13

Are you your brother's keeper?

Cain didn't think so, but then he's a poor example.

"No man is an island entire of itself," wrote the poet. The Bible says it a little differently: "None of us liveth to himself, and no man dieth to himself" (Romans 14:7). In our living we are responsible first to God, but we cannot ignore our fellow human beings.

God purposely created each of us as a social being. He did not design a world just for Adam and Eve. He gave them the power of procreation so that eventually the world would be full of people. We are all a part of what we call society. Anyone who thinks he can live in isolation is deceiving himself.

Unfortunately, the idea of becoming involved is shunned by many. "I'll live my life; you live yours" is a popular philosophy. It is not only impractical; it is unbiblical. The Bible has plenty to say about our social responsibilities. Jesus himself was emphatic on the subject.

In serving others we actually serve ourselves. This is why practicing what we call the Golden Rule makes us happy and helps us in every area of life.

Help, Don't Hurt!

Jesus spent a lot of time correcting the misinterpretations of the Law promoted by the religious leaders of Israel. His listeners kept hearing Him say, "Ye have heard . . . but I say unto you."

An Old Testament verse frequently misapplied in Jesus' time is often taken out of context today. It contains the expression "an eye for an eye, and a tooth for a tooth." People still assume this is justification for revenge, but even under the Law that wasn't God's intent.

When God established the Law He sought to prevent man's inhumanity to man. So He ordered punishment for those who might physically abuse another, at the same time limiting the degree of retribution (Leviticus 24:19-21). Today we speak of it as punishment to fit the crime. This was a strong incentive to refrain from violence. If the man who blinded another's eye or knocked out his tooth knew the same things would happen to him, he would be more inclined to hold his temper—as would the man who felt he could exact any penalty when he was wronged.

The people of Jesus' day failed to see that the purpose of this law was to prevent cruelty and injustice. They interpreted it only as justification for revenge. Jesus not only rejected such an interpretation, He also forbade any form of retaliation among His followers. His command is, "Resist not evil."

The obedient disciple of Jesus does not resist the evil man who strikes him. Instead, he turns his left cheek to the violent person who has slapped him on the right cheek.

Not all slaps are made with the hand. Some are made with the tongue! Blows may come as various kinds of mistreatment, including being cheated in financial matters. The principle Jesus laid down concerning nonre-taliation applies to all kinds of slaps.

What's the Alternative?

What can happen when violence is met with violence? Only greater violence, injury, and hatred. Each time retaliation occurs the other person is determined to respond with something stronger. The situation intensifies and sometimes the final results are tragic.

When a Christian meets evil with evil, he is adopting the tactics of the world—the world he is supposed to be trying to win for Christ. It is difficult to witness to someone when you have returned his slap with one of your own. On the other hand, a gentle response often makes the other person ashamed.

But what if all our attempts to follow Jesus' principle of retaliation bring us nothing but heartache and trouble? What if the other person only laughs at us and continues to take advantage of what he considers our easy-going attitude?

We will have the satisfaction that comes from obeying the Lord. We can commit matters into His hand, knowing that He can work them out far better than we can. Don't forget that Jesus promised a reward to those who suffer for righteousness' sake (Matthew 5:10). Receiving mistreatment because we obey His teaching certainly falls into this category.

Sometimes injustice does not involve violence. How is a Christian supposed to react to that? Paul answers in Romans 12:17-21. Stop and read this passage now. You'll find the principles the apostle lays down are identical with the teachings of Jesus—we are to defeat evil by doing good.

Sounds strange, doesn't it? It is so foreign to what we hear all the time that our first reaction is, "It just won't work." Why should a believer willingly give his coat to the man who threatens a lawsuit to take away his tunic—as Jesus said he should do? Since a Christian's life does not consist in the abundance of his material possessions (Luke 12:15), he willingly surrenders his possessions to those who demand them rather than becoming embroiled in a battle of insisting on his own "rights."

Anything that causes a Christian's testimony to suffer should be avoided. It is better to suffer loss than damage the cause of Christ (Philippians 3:8).

Roman law gave a soldier the right to compel a civilian to carry the soldier's gear for a distance of one mile. Jesus said, "Carry it two miles instead of one." Why?

The soldier would be surprised when a follower of Jesus carried his burden twice as far as required. (We can be sure he got a very different reaction from most people!) It is likely that the soldier would ask the Christian, "Why are you doing this?" The Christian could then share his testimony with the soldier with the hope that he would become a follower of Jesus too.

Do such opportunities for witnessing come through a Christian's "second mile" behavior today? Try it. You might be surprised.

Be Gracious—Jesus Was

Who can imagine Jesus being anything but kind, courteous, and thoughtful to everyone? The word *gracious* would certainly fit His actions. Can the same be said for us?

In Matthew 5:42 Jesus spoke to His followers about their dealings with nonbelievers. This is not a picture of Christians begging from other Christians. God's command to them is that they work and provide food for themselves (2 Thessalonians 3:10-12).

But when a non-Christian begs from a Christian, how

should the Christian respond? Jesus' answer is, "Give to him that asketh thee" (Matthew 5:42).

Again the underlying principle is that our first priority is to reach the unconverted for Christ. So when a Christian responds to one who begs from him, he seizes the opportunity to witness for Christ. He explains why he is willing to give—that Jesus has done a work of grace in his heart that causes him to love people. It is important that such a testimony be given along with the money. Otherwise the real meaning of the generosity is missed.

Immediately the question arises: "But what about the deadbeat, the professional who spends all his time taking advantage of others so he won't have to work?" We have all known Christians who were "taken" by people with a clever line, and it goes against the grain—no doubt about it. Yet this is a risk we must be willing to take in order to obey our Saviour and witness for Him. In the end God will see to it that we really do not lose anything. He will make it up to us—of that we may be sure. Our pride may be hurt by someone "conning" us, but that is part of the price of discipleship.

But What About Enemies?

Enemies—sometimes even Christians have them. If they are not the kind who try to harm us physically, they may at least be so hostile that they will leave no stone unturned to do us other kinds of damage. It may be through hurtful talk, outright lies, underhanded tactics on the job, or other diabolical schemes.

What is our responsibility as Christians in such situations? Again, Jesus' teaching goes far higher than any other. He commands, "Love your enemies."

Not only is there to be no retaliation by the Christian; he is to respond with the opposite kind of treatment. To those who act like enemies, the Christian is to show love.

When friends curse him, he is to respond by blessing—giving a soft answer (Proverbs 15:1) and wishing the other person the very best.

If the enemy's actions show downright hatred, the Christian answers by doing all the good and helpful things possible.

Surely we do not need an explanation of Jesus' expression, "despitefully use you." We have probably been "used" that way at some time—maybe often. How are we to respond? By praying for the other person, Jesus said. Above all, pray for his salvation.

"Average" Won't Do

We are inclined to measure ourselves by what we call "the average." If our conduct seems to be as good as most people's, we feel satisfied.

But Jesus is not content with followers who merely measure up to average human behavior. He wants to know, "Christian, what are you doing that is more than non-Christians do? How are you different from anyone else?"

The publicans (tax collectors) of Jesus' day were detested by others. Yet the publicans were capable of loving those who might happen to love them—probably just their own relatives. Jesus said His followers must exceed the conduct of the publicans. They must love those who return no love to them—and even hate them.

Even the heathen are capable of sharing greetings and warm wishes with their friends. Christians should do better than this. We should show ourselves friendly to those who are different from us.

Actually what Jesus taught is that we should imitate the God we worship. He loves the whole world. He doesn't restrict His sunshine and rain to the godly. He sends these blessings to the wicked so they will also have good crops. He sent His Son to die for sinners, and His Spirit constantly seeks them. Can we who are His children act in a different manner?

Jesus set the standard for His followers at absolute perfection—"even as your Father which is in heaven is perfect" (Matthew 5:48). Is this an impossible goal? Who can be perfect? God is, and Jesus will not have us trying to substitute a lesser pattern for ourselves than our Heavenly Father.

The word *perfect* in the original Greek means finished, complete. God's character cannot be improved, for it is complete. This is what His children are to aim at: completeness, wholeness of character. If we see points where we are weak we must not resign ourselves to the idea that "nobody's perfect." We must strive to strengthen those weak points until we become whole and complete in that area.

Obviously such perfection is unattainable if one is relying on human ability alone. But we are not. We are saved by the grace of God, kept by that grace, and led by it in our quest for perfection. The Holy Spirit helps us. We are strengthened by our study of the Word. It is a never-ending challenge—this pursuit of perfection. But it is worth all the effort.

We Are the Lord's

No Christian should be living exclusively for his own benefit and honor. We are all living under the lordship of Christ.

"Whether we live therefore, or die, we are the Lord's" (Romans 14:8). This is the basis for our conduct toward others, including our Christian brothers and sisters.

Most of us behave rather well when dealing with unsaved neighbors. We tend to be on guard if we know we are among enemies. But sadly, the place where some

Christians fail is in their relationship with other Christians.

Paul faced this problem in the churches of his day. Today the problem still exists, but perhaps in different guises.

It isn't necessary for Christians to be in agreement on every point. But we must recognize the price Jesus paid to save us all.

Paul knew that many Christians did not have the spiritual insights he had. Some were troubled by hang-ups about food, others about the observance of certain days. There were disagreements, but it did not mean there needed to be harsh debate.

Paul reminds us that we will all stand before the judgment seat of Christ. Each of us will give an account to God, including the way in which we have treated other Christians. If we have been harsh in our judgment of them, we will have to suffer the same kind of judgment (Matthew 7:1,2).

What does Paul mean when he talks about a Christian being a stumbling block to others? Simply this: If another Christian violates his conscience to copy my conduct, I have caused him to stumble. This is the basic teaching of Romans 14.

We must conduct ourselves in such a way that if a less mature Christian follows our example he will be helped, not hindered. We must never be so anxious to flaunt our convictions that others will be offended.

What a Christian does is not his business alone. None of us is an island—and who wants to be?

13

Citizens of Two Worlds

READ JEREMIAH 29:7; EZEKIEL 3:17; MATTHEW 22:17-21; 1 PETER 2:13-17

Since I am a citizen of heaven, how much responsibility do I have to the world I am now living in?

Citizenship is a great privilege. Paul said, "Our conversation is in heaven" (Philippians 3:20). "Conversation" actually means "citizenship." We are also citizens of our country. The Bible has clear teaching about responsibilities in both areas. We do not bear a good testimony to our heavenly citizenship if we are slothful about our earthly citizenship.

The world should be a better place because God's people are in it. Government from the lowest level to the highest should feel the influence of its Christian citizens. Jesus said we are the salt of the earth and the light of the world. We look forward to the day when we will shine in heaven, but we must start shining here.

It is unbiblical to ignore our role as citizens of our neighborhood, city, county, state, or nation. Our school system should be included too. We can influence these areas far more than we realize.

Government is ordained by God for the protection and well-being of the human race. It would be wonderful if rulers were always upright, God-fearing men. But despite the fact that often they are not, the offices they occupy are part of a system God has provided for the world. We must honor the offices even if we find the men less than admirable. God's people have often had to live under oppressive rulers. This is true in many areas of the world today.

Support Your Government

The Israelites had been carried away as captives to Babylon. Yet through His prophet God commanded them: "Seek the peace of the city whither I have caused you to be carried away captives, and pray unto the Lord for it: for in the peace thereof shall ye have peace" (Jeremiah 29:7). The *New American Standard Bible* translates the latter part of that verse, "for in its welfare you will have welfare."

The Israelites were not to think of themselves as prisoners of war dedicated to the overthrow of their conquerors. They were not to be filled with resentment and hatred toward those who ruled them.

Does it seem strange that the Lord told His people to pray for the evil heathen who ruled them? Why not pray instead for unrest and turmoil to torment them?

The logic in the Israelites' praying for the Babylonian government is found in the phrase, "for in the peace thereof shall ye have peace." Civil unrest often creates conditions that interfere with the propagation of the gospel. In some countries the work of missionaries has been severely hampered during times of civil disobedience, riots, and martial law. On the other hand, times of peace provide opportunities for the growth of the Church.

When a country enjoys stability and financial prosperity, the Church reaps the benefits because church members can find good jobs and contribute to the spreading of the gospel.

During times of political strife some politicians are looking for a scapegoat—some group to blame or persecute in an effort to distract attention from their own shortcomings. Sometimes churches are selected as targets for such diversionary persecution. Governments are usually more inclined to grant liberty to churches when things are going well.

Christians themselves can become taken up with political concerns during days of civil instability. This may lead to neglecting the primary duty of reaching the lost. The work of God fares better when those in the Church are not sidetracked by preoccupation with other matters.

This does not mean that God cannot bless His people in times of persecution and violence. Church history has shown that the gospel has made some of its greatest advances when Christians have been mistreated, imprisoned, and even murdered. God grants special grace to His people for these extreme situations. But it is not healthy for such conditions to continue indefinitely.

We read in Acts 9:31: "Then had the churches rest throughout all Judea and Galilee and Samaria, and were edified; and walking in the fear of the Lord, and in the comfort of the Holy Ghost, were multiplied." Here we see advancement by the Church because of tranquil conditions. We should pray that our government leaders will be given wisdom to solve the problems of governing so we may enjoy favorable conditions for our work in Christ's kingdom.

Oh, Those Taxes!

Running a government takes money, and much of that money comes from taxes. Regrettably, the tax burden is often unequal, and some people are experts at finding legal loopholes to avoid as much of their share as possible. This can be discouraging to law-abiding citizens, including Christians. There is a temptation to ask, "Why should I be paying when so many others are getting out of it?"

As long as we live in this sinful world, such inequities will exist. However, that does not mean taxes should be eliminated, or that Christians should follow the example of the ungodly in dealing with such matters.

Jesus indicated that God's people should pay their taxes to secular governments. The Pharisees resented every piece of money sent by the Jews to the heathen government that had conquered their land. The Herodians, although of Jewish birth, advocated full cooperation with the occupying Romans. These two divergent Jewish groups approached Jesus with a question obviously framed as a trap: "Is it lawful to give tribute unto Caesar?" (See Matthew 22:17.)

If Jesus answered yes, the Pharisees were ready to denounce Him as a traitor to Israel. If He said no, the Herodians could accuse Him of stirring up rebellion against the empire.

The result of this loaded question has benefited Christians ever since. Jesus made it clear that our secular responsibilities must be met. By paying taxes to governments ruled by evil men we are not compromising our loyalty to God. Indeed, Jesus said, "Render therefore unto Caesar the things which are Caesar's" (Matthew 22:21).

This means that Christ's followers should comply with all governmental requirements and regulations. This involves taxes, licenses, permits, fees, and other similar obligations. For a Christian to be surly or sullen about meeting his share of this financial burden is to fall short of Christ's expectations.

"For the Lord's Sake"

Peter lays down the principle of our obedience to government: "Submit yourselves to every ordinance of man for the Lord's sake" (1 Peter 2:13).

A Christian obeys the laws of his government for the Lord's sake—not because he likes the laws or the officials who enforce them. God is concerned that all men be saved, and if there is any one group the Lord especially wants to reach it is men in government. This includes kings (Acts 9:15), military leaders (Acts 10:22), governors (Acts 13:12; 24:24,25), and every other individual involved in such responsibilities.

Men of political power can remove barriers to the spread of the gospel. Thus the conversion of an official could influence many more to accept the message of Christ.

Christians, then, should do all they can to win the approval of government. This will give them an advantage in their work for the Lord. It may open doors that otherwise would be closed.

Christians must not compromise Biblical principles, however, just to win favor. If man's law and God's law conflict there is no question about which takes precedence for Christians. We must "obey God rather than men" (Acts 5:29). Let's just be sure, however, that it is God and His law we are following and not the rebelliousness of our own human nature.

Some men in authority have assumed that Christians are dangerous, unreasonable—perhaps mentally deranged. The best way to nullify such beliefs is for Spirit-filled Christians to live consistent, law-abiding, sensible, honest lives. Authorities will then be much more likely to respect and even admire those who profess to follow Christ.

Things will always be happening in government that we dislike. Fortunately our system provides for the citizen to express his will: through free speech, the vote, and other lawful forums. We must not, however, be caught up in the spirit that may bring change but is contrary to the Spirit of Christ. It puts things in a different light when you realize that you are conducting yourself soberly and respectfully for the Lord's sake. Proper behavior will do far more to convince men of the reality of the gospel than adopting the world's methods.

Be a Good Witness

God had something very important to say to His servant Ezekiel: "Son of man, I have made thee a watchman unto the house of Israel: therefore hear the word at my mouth, and give them warning from me" (Ezekiel 3:17).

The watchmen who patrolled the city walls were important men in those days. They were on duty through the night while others were sleeping and would sound the alarm if an invader was sighted. Ezekiel had to sound even more vital warnings to God's people: he had to warn them of spiritual dangers and rouse them to serve the Lord.

Christians today are also called to fill the role of the watchman. The world is lost and perishing. We must bring words of warning and hope. The responsibility rests on our shoulders.

The Great Commission is not just to pastors, evangelists, and missionaries; it is directed to every Christian: "Go ye therefore, and teach all nations, baptizing them in the name of the Father, and of the Son, and of the Holy Ghost: teaching them to observe all things whatsoever I have commanded you" (Matthew 28:19,20).

The Christian's message is better than Ezekiel's. We have the good news of forgiveness through Jesus Christ.

110

The gospel to which we bear testimony has the promise of God's indwelling presence for those who accept His Son. We have the message of the baptism in the Holy Spirit that equips God's people for witnessing. To the sick we can proclaim that Jesus heals. And with the hopeless, we can share the blessed hope—Jesus' return.

Jesus pictured the world as a field where two kinds of seed have been planted: the seed of evil and the seed of the gospel. Christians must not become so occupied with trying to uproot the tares (produced by the bad seed) that they forget their main task. Harvesttime will come and God will separate the tares from the wheat (Matthew 13:24-30). This task must be left to Him.

One day Jesus said to His disciples, "Lift up your eyes, and look on the fields; for they are white already to harvest" (John 4:35). We can easily become so busy with our own affairs that we forget a whitened harvest for which workers are greatly needed.

No one field is more important than another. Every nation must be reached with the gospel, but we must never forget that our witness starts at home. Dreams of going to a foreign land to spread the gospel will likely come to nothing if we presently ignore the lost in our own neighborhood.

The reassuring part of the Great Commission is the Lord's promise never to leave us alone in the harvest field. No single Christian can reach the entire world, but together—empowered for the task by our Lord—we can get the job done.

How Wonderful to Share

"The liberal soul shall be made fat: and he that watereth shall be watered also himself" (Proverbs 11:25).

Here is a principle that never fails. We cannot give

without having it given back to us. We cannot dispense blessing without having blessing returned to us.

Nobody wants to give to a stingy person. Every time he spurns a need, somebody knows about it. Conse-que...   ...away
whe...   ...iculty.

T... ...loved for
his ... ...or his kind-
ness, even though he may not be in need.

The Lord takes note of generous people too (Acts 10:4). Individuals and churches that give generously to spreading the gospel will testify that God prospers them as they give to His cause (Malachi 3:10). God intends to get the gospel to the entire world. He will see to it that those who are faithful in their stewardship will prosper.

Read Acts 4:32-35. After Pentecost, the Church grew and many of the newly converted Jews from other lands remained in Jerusalem. They yearned for more teaching about Jesus. They loved the newfound fellowship with other believers. This could have created a crisis in which people would have starved. But no one did. The Christians were filled with love and they shared whatever they had with others. This spirit of giving is seen throughout the New Testament.